tales from a
FORAGER'S
KITCHEN

the ultimate field guide
to evoke curiosity
& wonderment

Johnna Holmgren

RODALE.

RODALE
wellness

Live happy. Be healthy. Get inspired.

Sign up today to get exclusive access to our authors, exclusive bonuses,
and the most authoritative, useful, and cutting-edge information on health,
wellness, fitness, and living your life to the fullest.

Visit us online at RodaleWellness.com
Join us at RodaleWellness.com/Join

Follow us @RodaleBooks on 🐦 📘 📌 📷

We inspire health, healing, happiness, and love in the world.
Starting with you.

To my Bear, with my whole heart. Thank you for seeing me, hearing me, and believing in my ideas. Thank you for allowing me to be a wild forest fox and showing me what it means to be better and kinder every day. You are everything that's worth living for in this world. I love you so much, Max.

To my dearest daughters, Luella Beane, Minoux Wilder, and Juniper Eisley. There is no greater joy than to be a mother to you all! You remind me every single day to let go, be free, and fully experience the childlike wonder of being alive. You three are most curious, magical, and beautiful. I love you so much.

Contents

Introduction

I refuse to give in to the idea that once we reach adulthood, we must leave fascination and curiosity behind.

Imagine a child picking cattails by a lake just as they start to bloom and expand in pollen. Plucking each section of furlike pollen and throwing it in the air to join with the wind. To a child, the lake is so calm and the tails reach up almost as high as the clear sky. Over and over and over, she tosses the pollen. She is not thinking of what task needs to be completed next or what is due, when. There is so much happiness in her eyes, and she is completely present in that glorious magical moment. I want to bottle up this feeling and somehow pour it into our adult lives. If we could, I imagine we would be a much happier society. Wet and dripping in wide-eyed magic and wonderment for this life and giving ourselves permission to dream again and look at food and meals and the act of cooking and baking with such appreciation and amazement. It takes a lot of courage to be appreciative of this life and to reconnect with the bewitchment we all felt as children and be able to marvel at life as grown adults.

And yet, it's very easy to forget that there is magic in food. But just imagine if every day we tucked a small amount of appreciation and magic onto our plates? If we braided in a dash of adventure or tried something new in the simplest of forms?

What if we walked through the woods and spotted a textured brown morel or gathered a bountiful bouquet of Queen Anne's lace to cook a calming feast or preserve for the colder months ahead. Could we grasp this experience, bottle it up, and carry it with us throughout the week? It could make the mundane enchanting and maybe even make us a more appreciative by breaking our normal routine. Use fresh eyes when we walk the aisles of our co-op or grocery store to seek the obscure and allow ourselves to gravitate toward unexpected ingredient combinations. I'm intrigued with ingredients that nourish our bodies physically, but also nourish us mentally.

As a child with both a longing for nature and a tendency for sunburns, I picked up worms and injured birds and spent my days being fiercely devoted to the task of rescuing bunnies and salamanders out of our window wells as often as possible. I felt most alive when experiencing and connecting with the earth.

As time went on, growing up in the awfully cold and snowy state of Minnesota, I met a tall boy in school. For some reason, during those awkward years of 12 to 13, he was intrigued with my spunk, and I was equally captivated with his bundle of calm energy and alluring mind. Let's be honest: also with his tall, dark, and most handsome good looks. In seventh grade, I was obsessed with a combination of highlighter green

pants, a striped turtleneck, and a vibrant budding green vest. He was apparently into my monochromatic palette and slightly overbearing carbonated middle school persona.

I married the bundle of calm boy-turned-man named Max, but I call him my Bear. He eats like one, hibernates like one, and has a beard like one. He calls me his Fox because I eat like one, pounce like one, and curl up at night like one. He has accepted and encouraged me to be the wild foxlike creature that I am, letting me be free with dauntless projects and odd-ball ideas. On any given day, he would come downstairs or home from an illustration job to a newly painted bedroom, an experimental dish in the oven, branch curtains that draped over the living room table, or an extensive and detailed business plan for opening up a floral shop and café someday—one that serves really good food but includes a fresh bouquet of blooms with each of the dishes. Or something like that. His smile would soften and curve toward the sky while I'd verbalize all my plans and ideas. He'd pull me in for a hug or rub his hand over the top of my hair to mess it up and say, "Oh, you silly little fox, I love them. Also, I think something's burning."

We found out I was pregnant with our first little baby girl, Luella Beane, the day after we both decided to quit our jobs and pursue an entrepreneurial life of illustrating and photography. I began blogging, reading more books on foraging, documenting our life with a growing baby, and pressing "post" out to the Internet world. I wrote down stories of our world together, experiences with nature, and parenting and began a sort of catalog of new recipes that provoked wonder and whimsy inside of me. I named my blog *Fox Meets Bear,* and while it has changed over the years, it has been such an incredible space to be a part of. We had our second little girl, Minoux Wilder, in the fall, as the leaves began to change. She was born outdoors in the woods on my in-laws property, pine needles and all. Our third baby girl, Juniper Eisley, was born two falls later at our A-frame in the woods. Suffice it to say, life with our three sweet girls has been a beautiful and wild ride so far.

To be outdoors or walk through the woods during my earlier years was as essential as breathing for me. Rescuing animals and exploring with nowhere to be was simple. But I don't think anything or anyone quite prepares you for motherhood. The all-encompassing way it simultaneously

strips a woman down yet builds her up and adds new meaning to every corner and essence of life is astounding. It changed me from the inside out. The love for my girls fuels me on such intense levels, and there is no greater joy than to be their mother. Nothing will ever top that, and now I have six extra small hands to hold the corners of the branches for branch curtains. We experiment with ingredients together all throughout the week, and I have the permanent role of carrying all their foraged goods, collected rocks, and giant branches home after walks. To be in the kitchen cooking meals or baking goods for the Bear and them made me feel human again. It wasn't until I lost myself in motherhood, as some women do, that I actually ended up finding myself in a whole new way. I found myself there in the kitchen, standing with a sleeping child strapped to my chest and grasping goods from my own backyard. Slicing an ingredient that I'd never worked with before gave me the same feeling I felt when touching the soft fur of a deer hoof when I was in fourth grade. It filled me full of curiosity and wonder, and I longed to bring the same discovery and nourishment to the table for my family. When I nourished my mind as a mother, I was able to give more of myself to my little ones. I felt stronger and more satiated, both in body and mind. I began collecting my recipes and writing them down—trying things, failing at them, serving them to the Bear, and watching for his reactions. My curiosity was quickly matched by my willingness to fail.

In the late summer, we moved to an A-frame house in the woods that all four of our parents agreed was going to be a ton of work. With sweat and determination and the help of our parents and one incredibly talented older brother, we made it our own.

A brief seasonal summary of our life goes like this: After wearing layers of wool all winter long, we basically bathe in rain throughout the spring; then all through summer and fall, you'll find us in the woods, making stick shelters, weaving "floral" crowns made of weeds or flowers, or investigating a new type of moss or mushroom, studying whether or not it is edible. My daily normal is playing dress-ups with my girls, using up all the propane in the tank for baking and cooking, and every day hoping the septic system doesn't fail. We do a lot of family meditation and embrace many kinds of messes and emotions. I wholeheartedly believe that this life is meant to be experienced, felt, and embraced in most magical ways, and I am altogether drawn to seeking ways to bottle up the magic of the woods and carrying it into the kitchen.

There are those who have studied the art of foraging for most of their lives. There are countless published books that are filled cover to cover with categorical knowledge and specific regional information. I'm not here to offer that, repeat the charts, or pretend to be an expert on foraging. I am here, nestled in a home in the woods, cooking and baking for my family with foraged and earth-grown goods. These are my tales from a forager's kitchen.

WINTER   SPRING   SUMMER   FALL

Chapter 1

HOW TO USE
THIS BOOK

I believe in the idea that foraging can be experienced in the woods, on a roadside, or on top of a mountain, but it can also be experienced in a grocery store. You either picked up this book because you forage yourself or you are intrigued by foraging. But even if you don't live close to dirt or woods or rushing streams, you can still adhere to a forager's mind-set. A forager stays open to possibilities. A forager is drawn to the goodness of the earth. You can be a forager of the woods, but you can also be a forager at the farmers' market, hunting and gathering and letting your senses carry you to new small wooden cases of goods. You can even be a forager at the most conventional grocery store in the world. You can give yourself the freedom to break away from the norm and the mundane and create your own wonder, your own adventure, just by having the mind-set that something could be beautiful if you just open your eyes, see it, taste it, and experience it.

We have to give ourselves permission to be free and open to new possibilities on this earth!

Tales from a Forager's Kitchen consists of recipes, resources, supply lists, odes to earth-grown goods, intention and homage for connecting with the earth, and fairy tales for either yourself or your kids. This book is intended to be a practical guide to planting your own forest and cultivating sustainability and generosity for the woods, as well as a conglomeration of all things wild and free. It includes a combination of elements that intrigue me.

There are many ways to use this book just as there are many ways to do life. It can be read from cover to cover. It can stay in your kitchen. It can sit in your living room as a coffee table book. It can be flipped through and experienced at random. If you decide you hate it, you can use it for fire starter. It can be a source for learning about specific herbal aids and remedies or used as a field guide to foraging. I describe taste, touch, sound, sight, and smell and am drawn to magical realism. You can pull it out and read the short stories to your children while you bake a new recipe. You can gift it to the naturalist in your life or page through it while you wait for something to cook in the oven. This cookbook, to me, is like the ultimate field guide for curiosity in the kitchen. It's a reminder of how intensely life-giving it can be to connect with nature every single day in some way. It is a reminder to be open to spontaneity. If you're a planner, I hope it will remind you to plan time to be spontaneous.

Sit back and let the instructions take you from ingredient to ingredient at whatever pace suits you. Put this here. Add this there. It's okay to make notes inside of these pages, to flip each page with fingers dripping of honey or with dirt from a dandelion root. A book should be loved and used and engaged with as a fuel to help us have fresh eyes on familiar ingredients and give us the confidence to explore new ones.

All the food recipes yield for a family of four or five people. Some will have leftovers to be stored away for the next day or in glass jars to be frozen for a few weeks out.

The recipes should be altered or ingredients substituted to your liking. Connect with your preferred nuts or milk alternatives. This is a starting point to launch into different forms of exploration in the kitchen. It's a guide to look down at your plate and appreciate a meal that exemplifies sustenance. I've chosen ingredients that are wholesome and nourishing and provoke intrigue. I hope it makes you feel a little closer to moss and ferns and the feeling of the forest. I hope it gently nudges you to notice a ladybug in a new light. I hope it brings the woods to you among the taxis streaming by. I hope it feels like an invitation to escape to a different place!

I hope you use this cookbook to stoke your appreciation for the raw goodness of this earth. I consider it the antithesis of a weekly meal plan. It's more like a whisper to be brave and bold and try something new.

A FORAGER'S MANIFESTO

We believe in nature.

We believe in curiosity.

We believe in the beauty of the seasons. The mud, dirt, roots, berry-stained hands, slush, and summer-dripped sweat. We love all of the messes of each season and believe they are all good things.

We believe in small clippers and big baskets.

We believe that we are absolutely never too old to be bubbling with awe and a wide-eyed perspective for whimsy and wonder.

We believe in earth-grown goods!

We believe in the foraging mind-set. Being open to new experiences and new ingredients and new ideas, even if they exist one grocery aisle over.

We believe in God's goodness and the goodness of the Universe!

We are committed to the act of seeking fascination and wonder in the mundane.

We are committed to caring for this planet and harvesting responsibly.

A Forager's Mind-Set

By shifting our perspective toward foraging and being open-minded in the woods, we allow intrigue back into our lives. By having a forager's mind-set toward ourselves, our children, or others, we are able to experience an open-minded view of them. We are each on different journeys and paths; some are in rocky seasons of ups and downs, fallen trees, and winds that blow strong, while others are basking in the sunshine, with bounty growing at their feet and happiness overflowing. Both of these paths matter, and both of these scenarios can change at the blink of an eye.

In the woods, the elements can shift. I could hope for sun but instead encounter rain. I could prepare for wind and still be caught in a snowfall. I could plan for cool weather and end up stripping down layers to due the awakened heat of the sun. The same is with life, that we get so caught up in the ever-shifting elements around us, that we forget to breathe in the incredible parts of this earth.

We forget to stop and remember those childhood memories that so many of us have had that included some form of life-changing nature experience. We need to bottle that up and carry it with us into adulthood. I hope we can reopen that sense of childlike wonder and discovery and open-mindedness for the new and the magical and bring that into our kitchens and into the lives of our children or others. It can be so simple to connect with others' hearts and braid imagination and curiosity into our plates and our guests' plates. We can engage in imaginative conversation with others and open up an entire world of goodness and life-giving ingredients. We can gather from this earth, give back to this earth, and open up our eyes to see the glory in this life that we have been given. There is good on this earth. There are earth-grown goods available to us that can inspire our minds and hearts but ultimately nourish our bodies and souls so we are able to nourish others.

SUPPLY LIST: OUTDOORS

- An open mind

- Curiosity

- Basket for gathering (ideally two of them, one for unidentified edibles and one for identified edibles)

- Binoculars

- Bare feet or minimalist footwear

- Notebook and pen or pencil for documentation

- Water or hydration of choice

- Appropriate layers based on each season. There are always ways to prepare for a multitude of weather conditions.

- Harvesting knife. I prefer the Opinel pocket knife with a brush tip end for cleaning mushrooms and gently brushing off bugs.

A FORAGER'S WARDROBE

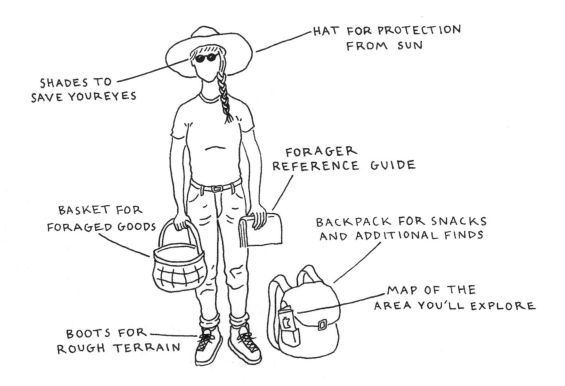

SHADES TO SAVE YOUR EYES

HAT FOR PROTECTION FROM SUN

FORAGER REFERENCE GUIDE

BASKET FOR FORAGED GOODS

BACKPACK FOR SNACKS AND ADDITIONAL FINDS

MAP OF THE AREA YOU'LL EXPLORE

BOOTS FOR ROUGH TERRAIN

SUPPLY LIST: INDOORS

- An open mind

- **THREE REALLY GOOD KNIVES AND AN HERB CHOPPER:** I have been cooking for my family, literally owning only three knives and one herb chopper. I believe that incredible dishes can be made, even if one doesn't have the fanciest, grandest collections. And that, my friend, is most refreshing. One serrated blade, one flat straight blade, one flat paring knife, and a rounded double-handed herb chopper will do.

- **STAINLESS STEEL SCRUBBER:** They wash a dish like no sponge can.

- **REUSABLE CLOTH COFFEE FILTER AND MUSLIN CLOTH TEA BAGS:** I use these to steep herbs and roots into stews and soups and to filter sap, kombucha, teas, and cocktails.

- **GLASS JARS IN ALL SIZES:** Mason jars, found and collected., are used for storing bulk herbs, ingredients, teas, and the mini-est of collectables.

- **APPLE CIDER VINEGAR PLUS APPLE CIDER VINEGAR WITH HONEY:** I use these a lot and believe in them with my whole heart. They are to a forager what flour and sugar are to a baker. The brand I recommend as most pure and authentically nourishing is Bragg. They offer numerous organic dressings, aminos, oils, and vinegars. Exceptionally top-notch!

- **BOB'S RED MILL GOODS:** An abundance of organic nut and seed flours and meals, grains, beans, seeds, oats, gluten-free mixes, and nutritional boosters. Their time-honored technique toward holistic and traditional stone milling is inspiring.

- **CAST-IRON PAN:** I use a variety of pans ranging from a beautiful set of copper pots and pans we received as a wedding gift, all the way to a single worn and beaten cast-iron pan that I've had for years and was used when I got it. It still sticks out to me as my favorite. To "season" this pan, it only needs to be rinsed in water and the food entirely scraped off. Never use soap and experience how it cooks each item of food. The added iron seeping into each meal is so good for us and adds incredible flavor to meats, mushrooms, or eggs.

- **HIMALAYAN SALT BLOCK:** Cooking in the kitchen or outdoors with a salt block is one of the prettiest, most magical processes! I prefer the 12-inch-wide by 8-inch-deep by 1.5-inch-high size for larger mushrooms and ingredients to sizzle. Individual himalayan salt stones are also used throughout this book for nourishing soups and for rebalancing the ph level through salted water. These can be found at many small holistic stores as well as at so many more stores these days, but if you don't find them in your area, there are numerous variations in sizes available online.

- **A ROCK AND A CUTTING BOARD OR A MORTAR AND PESTLE:** I use these for crushing herbs and edibles and bursting cloves of garlic wide open. There is something about crushing rock to herb that is beyond satisfying. Seeking out a favorite stone and storing it indoors creates such a sense of connection to the earth, even when inside.

- **OILS:** I prefer sunflower oil or coconut oil for their consistency, workability, and flavor. Many of the oils my recipes call for can be substituted with your preferred oil.

Foraging Etiquette

Whether you're foraging through tall magical woods, a grassy roadside, or suburban or city land, there is an unwritten code with a few simple guidelines to adhere to.

- Only forage what you plan on consuming. It's easy to be entranced by a patch of blooms or bursting burrows of fungi, but collect only what you need and leave the rest for others, whether they may be humans or animals. There is a beautiful kind of cycle and flow that happens when we actively consider those around us. Gratitude is essential. Be sure to give the edibles a simple form of thankfulness and appreciation for its root system, leaves, color, and nourishment.

- A slow-harvesting approach increases the connection to the plant, animal, or earth-grown good. Take care of the ground below and around the foraged good. Snip florals and blooms straight with clippers or a foraging knife. Don't tear. Fold back layers of dirt and tuck back the earth how you found it. Be conscious of your location of foraging.

- Many times roadsides or lawn-side areas are sprayed with chemicals, pesticides, or fertilizers or doused in car exhaust. Be aware of this and forage farther into the woods if possible, wash the edibles carefully, or choose to pass on the edibles—all make a difference in what nourishes the body.

- Be sure to ask permission if you are harvesting on someone else's land. There is beauty in experiencing something with another person, so don't be afraid to ask them to join you. Perhaps they haven't thought about the edibles growing on their land and would want to take part.

- Each state park and state forest has specific guidelines about what can or cannot be harvested. In my area, it is permissible to pick things such as edible fruits, edible nuts, wild mushrooms, wild asparagus, and watercress for personal consumption but is not acceptable to pick seeds, wildflowers, rocks, or minerals or to uproot anything. Be sure to research your local area and demonstrate an equal respect for the land and for those who care for it.

- Take your time and offer intention toward learning about each edible. Be unafraid to perform grown-up "book reports," in which you study the habitat or the edible. Learn its qualities and root systems, how and when it grows best. Document your findings. Be certain that you are 100 percent sure of the species and their identification before consumption. Some species will simply give you an upset stomach, but others, especially in the fungi world, can be so dangerous and their potency so strong that it may lead to death. If you aren't 1 million percent sure, don't eat it.

- Pick up litter when you see it! Dispose of it properly. Care for this earth by teaching your children to be mindful of garbage, recycling, and proper litter disposal.

- Plant edibles in your yard or land or on a sunny windowsill.

- Research your state park's Volunteer Day and teach your children to give back to the earth in small ways like planting wild grasses or wildflower bombs.

- Engage with local foraging resources to seek reputable sources within your direct region to give you a basis for your explorations through each season. Support restaurants that support those who forage for a living. Sources such as "Identify That Plant" online offer a comprehensive list of foragers and authors with published resources, links to their blogs if present, and geographical regions for each individual.

GARLIC CHIVES
Have a pleasant garlic flavor;
long used in Oriental cooking

SAVORY
Beans, vegetables, meats,
pastas, rice, leaves used in tea

Chapter 2

BREAKFAST

Scrambled Egg Trout

2 filleted fresh whole trout

3 tablespoons olive oil, plus more for drizzling

Salt block

1 cup seasonally foraged mushrooms such as chanterelles or oysters

½ cup fresh bouquet lavender

6 to 8 eggs

2 tablespoons butter

2 tablespoons apple cider vinegar with honey (Braggs Apple Cider Vinegar with Honey Blend "with the mother"), plus more for drizzling

1 cup whole blackberries

Salt

Black pepper

½ cup strawberries

1 cup live micro greens or dandelion greens

My dad took us fishing every single summer when I was a little girl. I didn't realize it when I was younger, but as I got older, I recognized just how patient he was and how much time he gave to the four of us kids. He didn't even get to fish himself for at least the first 2 hours. He alternated between setting up the lines, re-knotting the hooks, replacing the bobber, getting the worms out, worming the lines for my younger sister, taking a teeny catch off the line, rebaiting, relining, and pulling the hook out from some stuck seaweed.

My dad was the one to teach me how to fillet a fish and to this day, I can visualize his step-by-step process. This recipe brings me right back to that feeling of happiness and connection with each other and is by far my favorite breakfast dish. We fished in both the winter and the summer and froze what we caught in the freezer to pull out for breakfast, lunch, or dinner. Fish fries were a yearly occurrence with my cousins and aunts and uncles and the memory is so strong, I can almost taste the fish from years past. The comforting feeling of laughing and playing with my cousins in the backyard as my grandma set up the food, and the Minnesota air felt so warm.

There are so many reasons why I am utterly intrigued and infatuated with this recipe. I love the way the blackberries pop and drip and drizzle when baked, and I love the hint of fresh lavender and the way the leaves feel like sweet edible velvet in my mouth. The trout falls apart with the gentlest fork into the meat and is paired with a buttered, honey-scrambled egg. The olive oil soaks into it all and makes for a most moist meal to begin the day. A fish feast.

Prepare the trout first on a flat tray lined with parchment paper. Once the fish are filleted and ready, lay them open and drizzle with olive oil. Brush the oil on or simply glaze and drip.

Then, set up the stove. Then stack two of your stovetop grates on top of each other double high, and place the salt block on top. Turn on low to slightly medium heat to begin warming the stone. Sprinkle a few drops of water on the block. If they sizzle vigorously and disappear immediately, the block is ready.

Brush off any dirt and chop the stems off the mushrooms. Lay them in a straight line on top of the salt block, leaving space on the left-hand side of the block. Drizzle with barely any olive oil! One small streak up the center of your fungi'd line will do. This creates a beautiful absorption of the salt from the block and keeps the mushrooms slightly moist during the process.

Pull the leaves from the stem of the lavender and chop them in small, tiny pieces. Set aside.

The mushrooms should be sizzling now, and they will need to be turned just like the "There's three in the bed and the little one said, roll over" story. Flip the first mushroom to the left with a fork and then so on and so on, shifting each one down. This way, each side will be simmered and sizzled.

Preheat the oven to 350°F. Melt the butter and the apple cider vinegar with honey into a large flat pan over medium heat. I promise, the taste of this will change the way you make scrambled eggs forever! Crack open the eggs and swiftly fork them in low, small circles. Cook the eggs until they are just close to being done and you see slight dripping wetness around the edges; then turn the heat off (they will finish cooking in the oven). Take half of the eggs and lay them gently into the "bottom" half of one fish, covering the meat. Repeat on the other fish. Next layer half of the mushrooms fresh off the hot salt block on top of the eggs. Layer, tuck, and sing sweet melodies as you squish them into their soft egg-ed bed. Do the same for the other fish. Plop fresh blackberries and chopped lavender onto the eggs. Dust with salt and pepper.

Take the top of each fish and pull down and over to fold on top of the eggs. Slide two strings, about 8 to 10 inches long, under each of the fish and tie in a simple bow. One should be toward the head and one toward the tail, sealing the fish. Add fresh chopped lavender, any extra berries or strawberries to be baked. Drizzle olive oil on top of the closed-up fillets and lay a sheet of parchment paper over the two fillets. Bake for 15 to 17 minutes or until fish flakes apart easily with a fork. Take off the parchment paper to cook for an extra 2 minutes, which should brown the tops of the fillets ever so nicely.

Serve with a bursting side of live micro greens or dandelion leaves topped with fresh strawberries and blackberries. Spritz with apple cider vinegar with honey as a light dressing.

Star Anise Porridge

4 cups water

5 to 7 whole star anise

1/4 teaspoon anise seeds

2 1/2 cups whole rolled oats

1 tablespoon sprouted
buckwheat

1 tablespoon sprouted
chia seeds

1/2 tablespoon golden
flaxseeds

1 tablespoon rainbow
quinoa

1/2 teaspoon cinnamon

1/2 teaspoon ginger

Magical mornings begin with an enchanting breakfast. The only thing missing here will be Goldilocks and her three bears and it is bound to turn mornings of cereal into a most fairy-tale-like dish. This one isn't just for kids, either. Indulge in the warmth of this dish and notice the way the star-shaped anise settles into the bowl. Star anise is the fruit of an evergreen plant called *Illicium verum* and is dripping in hints of licorice flavor. This healing herb is filled with wholesome goodness and is a star-bursting form of antioxidants. Document and notice this shape in the earth.

The licorice root flavor can be foraged by seeking wild fennel in the late fall to gather, freeze, and store the seeds in a jar for use for up to a year. Anise hyssop leaves can be gathered and steeped in hot milk to add a spicy licorice flavoring, and additionally the petals can be dried and used as a replacement for star anise here.

Heat the water in a pan until it begins to simmer. Tuck the anise stars and seeds into an herb bag and simmer in the water for 10 minutes or until it begins to boil. If you are using wild fennel or fresh anise hyssop flowers or leaves, steep like a tea in almost boiling milk for 5 to 7 minutes—longer if you prefer a stronger blend like I do. Stir in the rolled oats, buckwheat, chia seeds, flaxseeds, quinoa, cinnamon, and ginger. Simmer on medium heat for about 10 minutes, stirring occasionally. Leave the bag in the pot to continue to steep.

Pour the finished contents into a bowl and top with an extra dash of cinnamon, brown sugar, peanut butter, raw wildflower honey, or cream-top whole milk. It's most magical to top with a star anise fruit and serve with a whimsical outlook. Add nuts to your liking! Serve on a giant wooden board or tray and pair with a warm beverage, linen napkin, fresh blooms, and wooden animal or handwritten note as a simple way to create magic for yourself or those you are serving. A from-the-woods breakfast in bed.

Pheasant Toast

4 tablespoons duck fat oil

Wild foraged pheasant
or chicken breast

8 ounces raw aged
cheddar

6 slices sprouted bread

Alder smoked salt

Smoked pepper

Almost nothing compares to the captivating texture and color palette of the pheasant. Their feathers are like a magic eye maze that draws you in until new shapes and forms are recognized. A dish prepared with partridge or pheasant has been linked scientifically to improvements in mood and alleviation of depression due to the traces of selenium. Not only does it just "feel" good to eat nutritionally dense meats, but it also actually physiologically changes the body's production of chemical and hormones toward the better. Pheasant has an underlying taste of wild, but is similar to a white chicken meat and when cooked right, makes an excellent start to the day. If you don't have access to pheasant in your area, a tender chicken breast is an excellent substitute. Duck fat is an incredible spread to use due to the lack of processing that it undergoes. While most cooking fats and oils are treated with chemicals, as well as bleached, deodorized, and refined, duck fat is simply rendered, or gently "melted" away from the flesh. This creates a healthy cooking fat in its purest form!

Add 1 tablespoon of duck fat to your pan. Slice the pheasant or chicken in small, thin strips and heat over medium heat. Be sure to flip the pheasant and brown on both sides; wild game should generally be on the rare side rather than well done as that makes for a more tender bite and better flavor. Slice the raw aged cheddar into thin slices and set aside as the pheasant finishes up. Pop your bread in the toaster oven or warm it in a pan on both sides. Once the bread is toasted, spread the additional duck fat on all pieces; use more if you prefer a juicier toast experience. Layer on the cooked pheasant, the raw cheddar, then the salt and pepper to taste. Devour.

NOTE: The best pan to use for this is a cast-iron one due to the way it browns each side of the pheasant evenly. Cooking with cast iron also increases your iron intake. Win, win! You can also take these types of pans into the outdoors for a fire-top cook.

Wild Blueberry Bee Pollen Scones

1⅓ cups all-purpose flour

1 cup Bob's Red Mill ivory wheat flour

6 tablespoons raw cane sugar

2 teaspoons baking powder

1 teaspoon baking soda

Pinch of salt

¾ cup whole milk yogurt

¼ cup whole milk or half-and- half

1 teaspoon vanilla

6 tablespoons butter (a little more than half a stick), room temperature

Dollop of honey

Dollop of maple syrup

1 tablespoon bee pollen, plus more for topping

1½ cups whole rolled oats

¾ cup frozen wild blueberries

Maple Whipped Cream (page 23)

An all-in-one bowl glorious scone pie. These can be balled out and made as individual scones, tucked into a buttered muffin pan, or baked as flat disklike cakes. There's something extra special about pulling a cakelike shape hot out of the oven to serve to others, so this is always my go-to when I am drawn to making things feel a little fancier or more special. Throw a beeswax candle on top for a morning birthday celebration or afternoon merriment. Observe the bursts of wild blueberries as they erupt open with the slice of the fork. Pop! pop! pop! Ivory wheat flour gives breads a light, golden color and has a sweeter flavor than conventional whole-wheat flour, so it appeals to those who find whole wheat baked goods to be slightly bitter. Like regular whole-wheat flour, Bob's Red Mill's ivory wheat flour will make baked goods denser. To achieve a lighter texture, try a 50-50 combination of all-purpose flour and ivory wheat flour. You can also substitute the ivory wheat flour with almond flour, cattail flour, or any other alternative flour of your choice.

In one bowl, mix both flours, raw sugar, baking powder, baking soda, and salt until evenly woven. Add in the yogurt, milk or half-and-half, vanilla, butter, honey, maple syrup, and bee pollen. Once all the ingredients are combined, spoon in the oats gently. Fold in the blueberries with a spoon. Spoon out the dough in flat circular disks on a sheet pan lined with parchment paper, each about 2 inches in diameter, leaving room on the edges for expansion.

Bake at 350°F for 15 to 18 minutes or until browned on top. Sprinkle with a handful of raw bee pollen just after taking fresh out of the oven, so they sink into the warmed parts and latch on. Let cool for 15 minutes before serving. You can serve them plain, with fresh berries on the side, or with Maple Whipped Cream followed up with a handful of bee pollen sprinkles. Magic!

MAPLE WHIPPED CREAM

½ pint heavy whipping cream

½ cup powdered sugar

1 tablespoon maple syrup, plus more for drizzling

¼ teaspoon vanilla

Bee pollen

Combine the cream, sugar, maple syrup, and vanilla. Chill the bowl in the freezer for 10 minutes. Then whisk! Whip it good! Sprinkle with bee pollen on top and a drizzle of fresh maple syrup. Serve! Store the extra whipped cream in a sealed container in the fridge where it will last for about 5 days!

Perspective

The same recipe, baked differently, gives off three separate completed dishes. It summarizes the power of perspective. Say you take the same exact amount of flour, sugar, blueberries, and oats to compile a scone recipe, yet you bake one third of it in a buttered muffin pan, another third in round balls on top of a sheet pan, and the other third formed into a disc-like shape on top of parchment paper—you get three different experiences. In life, there are "good and bad" things that happen to us, yet it all comes down to perspective and how we view things. This, to me, is so important to braid into how we are living. It's all the way we view things and the words in which we choose to form and speak to describe a scenario. Someone's wild adventure is another's complete boredom or biggest fear. I love that. I love that this scone reminds me of that. We are all wired so completely differently, and we all bring our pasts to the table, our experiences, our hurts, our views of life. The way in which we see life equates to our happiness and our fulfillment and our contentedness. That idea has stuck with me for so long. Mind-set matters.

Relativity, proportion, viewpoint, the angle, our curiosity, one's timeline, our capacity for growth, our definition of good or bad—they all matter and all group together to create our outlook on others or ourselves, I believe. Whenever I make this scone recipe, I think of that and how there is always more than one way to observe and engage with ourselves and others and the world.

Fungi Pancakes

1 cup oat flour

1 cup organic ivory wheat flour

2 tablespoons raw turbinado sugar

2 tablespoons flaxseed meal

1 teaspoon salt

¼ cup coconut or sunflower oil

2 eggs

2 teaspoons vanilla

Splash of milk

¼ teaspoon cinnamon

3 tablespoons finely chopped shiitake mushrooms (use what is forgeable and in season if possible)

Vegetable, canola, or sunflower oil

Paprika or turmeric and cinnamon

Several sprigs of rosemary

Maple syrup

Grass-fed butter

Maple Whipped Cream (see page 23)

Red reishi mushroom powder

This is an alternate version of my grandpa's famous pancake recipe—the one I grew up having on most Saturday mornings in my family, minus the oat flour and flaxseed and mushrooms. It's all about the drama with pancakes. Shape them as mushrooms, add fresh greens or herbs for grass and a dollop of whipped cream as fluffy clouds, and don't be afraid to break out the gnome and fairy books.

Mix the flours, sugar, flaxseed meal, salt, oil, eggs, vanilla, milk, cinnamon, and red reishi mushroom powder in a bowl. It doesn't matter how or when, just get them all in there. I mean, these are pancakes we are making here! Toss the mushrooms into the batter. Begin to heat up the pan on the stove and gently drip in a thin layer of vegetable, canola oil, or sunflower oil—these are lighter and thinner oils that will not burn as easily! The heat should be around medium to high.

Begin by imagining the shape of your mushroom pancake, starting to spread the batter from the base of the mushroom up to the cap. Remember the batter will expand, so give yourself enough room for the batter to crawl out to the edges of the pan! As it cooks on one side, sprinkle either the paprika or turmeric on the top of the cap and the cinnamon on the stalk of the mushroom. Watch for the batter to begin to burst with bubbles, then flip when the bubbles are even. Be open-minded! It's okay if the first one doesn't turn out—they almost NEVER do. It's a forever lesson to try, try again, even with only a pancake. I believe in you.

Serve on a plate with a sprig of rosemary, fresh maple syrup, loads of grass-fed butter, and homemade whipped cream.

Good Morning Greens

1 cup arugula

1 cup green oak lettuce

Bouquet of foraged and fresh dandelions

¼ cup fresh or frozen elderberries

Wild blackberries

Wild strawberries

Raw cheddar cheese

2 boiled duck eggs

Black pepper

Salt

Duck Salad Dressing (see page 235)

Dandelion leaves are used often in traditional Chinese medicine and offer support to our liver, nourish our bones and joints, while simultaneously cleansing our urinary systems. Every part of the dandelion is useful. Plus it gets you outdoors right away in the morning to forage, which is always a breath of fresh air, literally. The fresh greens nourish the morning with deep green goodness, and the richness of the duck eggs sits well in the belly, forming a sense of energy to carry one through the morning. A duck egg has twice the amount of protein than a chicken egg. Arugula carries vitamin C, vitamin A, folate, and calcium through us.

This is a very simple, cleansing breakfast that starts the day with abounding nourishment and earth-grown goods resting in the belly. It is a single-plated recipe. For serving more, double or triple this recipe.

Wash the arugula, lettuce, dandelions, strawberries, and blackberries under cold water and let air-dry while pulling the small, bursting-with-color elderberries from the stem. The stems are not to be eaten so be sure you are only consuming the berries! Layer your plate with greens, elderberries, blackberries, and strawberries, and add strips or squares of raw cheddar cheese. Crack open your boiled eggs, slice them in half, and cover with heavy pepper and light salt. Drizzle the salad dressing over all.

NOTE: Scrambled duck eggs are so insanely amazing but sometimes there's not enough time in the morning to watch a scramble, so I prefer to boil duck eggs ahead of time for the week ahead. So, if you're a plan-ahead type of human, grab your chilled cooked egg from the fridge and a nice big plate and pile the greens and sliced egg over the whole thing.

Once Upon a Maple Syrup!

It was February 15, the earliest that the maple syrup season has come in well over 10 years, which means the warm weather came early, too! It was the end of our first winter at the A-frame. We made it. Nothing huge broke down and spring was arriving soon. The propane tank was full and it had me longing to cook. The birds began to chirp more, and I even found one mosquito inside our house in February! I have absolutely no idea how it got in there, except that we had left all the windows open. It was a sure sign of warmer weather, so I welcomed it in (kind of).

Our neighbors have been living on Grey Cloud Island for many years and have been tapping the trees on our property since their kids were little. We got to meet them all, and they walked us through the whole process of tapping for maple syrup—it was so magical. The taps were tucked into the lines of the bark on the tree and the sap dripped out so fast. It was definitely time. The first night there were about 5 cups of sap in the bag and by the next night there were well over 15. The taps stayed on the trees for the next few weeks. From a ratio perspective, most sap is 2 percent sugar, and it takes 43 gallons of sap to make 1 gallon of maple syrup! Forty-three gallons harvested, lifted from bucket to bucket to boiling pot to be boiled down. It is such a beautiful ode to slowing down life and appreciating the most simple things. I was so intrigued.

Sap officially becomes maple syrup when it reaches 66.9 percent sugar. The magic moment is measured as it boils on the stove and reaches 7°F above the boiling point of water. When boiling sap reaches 219°F, that means enough water has been removed to make it officially maple syrup. Maple trees run sap the best if the tree goes through a freeze/thaw cycle. It is all based specifically on the wind, sun, and tempera-

ture that season. The other way that maple trees produce sap best is when the trees are tapped just before the active growing season. Once the trees leaf out and begin to grow actively, they heal very quickly and the holes that were drilled dry up and heal over.

I boiled my first small batch indoors. I burned the first batch when I tucked the girls into bed and came out to my husband flagging out more smoke than I'd ever seen. Whoops! I boiled my second batch the next morning, which ACTUALLY turned out, and it was so rewarding, I can't even explain. No wonder maple syrup costs an arm and a leg. It's definitely worth it when calculating the amount of time and energy it takes to create just 1 gallon.

By February 28, the syrup bags were so full that they were falling off the trees. The bags filled up and expanded and were firm to a finger poke. I almost considered lapping up the small puddles that had dripped onto the ground below the bag, but decided to leave the sweet nourishment to the newly sprung bugs and the forest floor. I spent the entire day boiling down the sap and making so much syrup, I didn't know what to with it all. I emptied bag after bag into jars and bowls and pots and pans and even filled up an enormous tub. My friends came over and gathered some sap of their own. Then the next day, March 1, we awoke to snowfall! The biggest flakes were falling and at least 4 inches of fresh cold cotton fluffed puff was on the ground. The sap bags each had a stack of frozen alabaster flakes on their top layer and the innards of the bag had turned to a frozen slush that reminded me of a slushy at the State Fair growing up. The light of sunshine crept out again midmorning, like another tease of spring. The sap production sped up once again. The bags filled and I found myself again pouring the sap into any containers I could gather from around the house, dividing it into glass jars and empty pots and feeding the girls sips of raw, fresh sap in between pours. Then I finished by re-hanging the bags to fill up again. I boiled down sap in small individual batches over the whole next week and into the weekend. Gifted

more sap to my friends, and the trees continued to spill their liquid until mid-March!

There was a point in this process where I spilled a few teaspoons of maple syrup on the counter from my very first batch, and I may have slurped it up fresh off the marble counter.

I just had to get that out there.

It is a sublime way to close the chapter on winter and welcome the coming spring; this was just the first of many more years of this tradition for us as a family. My husband does an absurdly amazing impression of me at 85 with hearing loss from playing my music too loud in my headphones, and I imagine myself as that Grandma someday, rocking in some worn denim overalls with a light wool sweater, teaching anyone who wants to listen to the process of tapping a maple tree for maple syrup. Basically, major goals for my life.

HOW TO TAP A MAPLE TREE

*Drill (brace) with ⁷⁄₁₆"
or ³⁄₈" drill bit*

*Spiles or tapping spouts
(Spiles can be made or
purchased and come in
materials such as wood,
aluminum, or plexiglass)*

Hammer

*Bag or bucket to collect
sap*

A sugar maple is the most popular tree to tap due to the high concentration of sugars. These trees could be defined as the most generous trees of all, in terms of sap production and sugar release. The tree should be at least 10 inches in diameter before it can be tapped. If it's over 18 inches, you can put two taps into its trunk. If it's more than 28 inches, you can put three taps into its trunk, dispersing them evenly around the trunk about waist high. Drill into the tree at least 1.5 to 2 inches deep with the drill and release back to you, pulling out the shavings and bark. Insert the spile and use a hammer to gently secure it into the tree tightly. Connect the bag to the spile. Wait and watch the sap fill.

HOW TO BOIL THE SAP

*Collection containers—
plastic buckets, milk jugs,
or glass jars work well*

*Cheesecloth, mesh
strainer, coffee filter,
or glass filter*

*Large pot (use a 5- to
8-quart size if you plan
on boiling down small
batches indoors. For
boiling down over a fire
outdoors, use a large,
low, and broad pan)*

Spoon

Small pot

Candy thermometer

Jars with canning lids

Harvest the sap as it fills the bag or bucket. It's best to boil it down as soon as you can after collecting it off the tree, but it can be stored in the refrigerator for up to 7 days to avoid any bacteria growth.

Strain the fresh sap through cheesecloth, a mesh strainer, coffee filter, or glass filter into a large 5- to 8-quart pot. If you plan on cooking a large portion of sap at one time, then the preferred method is over an outdoor fire. But the sap can be evaporated indoors if it is a smaller batch (under a few quarts of sap). It would be a good idea to crack a window or turn on your exhaust fan. This is due to the high amounts of moisture that is released from the sap as it boils down to the sugar. Watch for the sap to turn to a caramel-like color. Using a spoon, skim off foam and bubbles as they build up and discard them! Boil until it reaches the golden color and then move it to a smaller pot for the final boiling. Use the candy thermometer to track the sap temperature. The temperature needs to reach 7°F over the boiling point of water. This varies with elevation.

Pour into sterilized canning jars, leaving headspace, and cover with sterilized lids. Boil in boiling water bath for 10 minutes to seal the lids. Remove the jars and store at room temperature.

When buds begin to form on a tree or the temperature stays above freezing, it's time to stop collecting sap!

Next step: Host a pancake party.

Foraged Mushroom and Charcoal Cinnamon Rolls

There was a certain time one January, when the temperature changed and the snow hadn't fallen in a few days but there was still this fresh white carpet laid on the ground. I was out walking and could not believe the color of the trees. They were as black as the deepest, darkest layer of black. Each single tree seemed to be wrapped in a blanket of velvet, as if someone had physically tucked them in for the duration of the last few months of cold. I don't know if it was the moisture in the air mixing with the time of day that I hiked, but it was mind-blowing. Each trunk so contrasted with the ground. Alive and strong and bold. It reminded me of deep, mysterious black charcoal. It sinks into my skin so deeply and stains my hands with the most charming cloudlike sensation. I am so intrigued with cooking and baking with black charcoal. It's something I've incorporated into my diet for the last few years for aiding any stomach ailments and is what I reach for at the first sign of queasiness or sickness—it's my actual magic potion pill.

Charcoal is incredibly cleansing and nourishing and travels into the body to rid of toxins or bacteria. The absorption is the reaction of elements, including nutrients, chemicals, and toxins, soaked up and assimilated into the blood stream. Adsorption is the chemical reaction where elements bind to a surface. The porous surface of activated charcoal has a negative electric charge that causes positive charged toxins and gas to bond with it. The nooks and crannies in activated charcoal are created through a heating process, which in turn aid in healing the gut. Short story—it is both sweet and savory, nourishing and cleansing.

You'll need a loaf of sweet dough to start this recipe. Home-made dough is so good and honestly so simple. It freezes really well, so you can pull it out at any time the night before or even morning of, at the crack of dawn when those little lives wake up. In this recipe, the mushrooms counter the sugar crash that normally accompanies a cinnamon roll experience, leaving you with a sustained and nourished discovery.

recipe continues

1 batch Sweet Foxie
Dough (see below)

1 stick butter, softened

1 to 2 cups chopped
mushrooms (white
button, shiitake, or forest
nameko are my favorite)

3 tablespoons goat cheese
(cream cheese is also
incredible)

1 cup raw turbinado sugar

1/2 cup brown sugar

1 tablespoon cinnamon

1/4 teaspoon ground cloves
(optional)

1 tablespoon charcoal
powder

Roll out the dough in a square formation, leaving the edges thin but not breakable. Begin to spread the butter—the rule is you have to just use your hands. Get in there and apply the butter evenly to that sweet dough. Lay the chopped mushrooms over it and spread them evenly over the whole square. Plop dollops of goat cheese evenly! Sprinkle sugars, cinnamon, and cloves, if using. End by sprinkling the charcoal powder evenly over the entire square.

Preheat the oven to 350°F. Butter your cinnamon roll pan. So many good options here—I've made them in mini loaf pans, petite copper ware, full sheet-size pans, and round cake pans.

Begin to roll the edge that's closest to you, gently pulling it toward you with each tug, and continuing to roll all the way toward the opposite edge to make a nice long tube. Take a knife and begin to make slices into the tube, about 2 or 3 inches wide, but again adapt to what type of pan you have. Play around—cuts of varying widths make for big and small rolls.

Layer the slices in the pan and sprinkle additional charcoal powder on top. Bake for 27 to 30 minutes. Check in on them and remove when the edges are browned to your liking. Since activated charcoal powder is going to be entering the body to rid of toxins, don't forget to drink a big glass of water with this recipe. Extra bonus points if you forage your own mushrooms.

SWEET FOXIE DOUGH

2 3/4 cups whole wheat
flour (can substitute acorn
flour, all-purpose, coconut
flour, or almond flour)

1/2 cup pure cane sugar

3/4 teaspoon salt

1/2 teaspoon ground cloves
(optional)

1/2 cup whole milk

4 tablespoons butter,
room temperature

1 large egg yolk

1/4 cup wild yeast

1 heaping tablespoon
raw honey

Combine the flour, sugar, salt, and cloves, if using, in a bowl. Warm the milk just slightly and add to the bowl along with the butter, egg yolk, and wild yeast. Mix with your hands or in a mixer until combined. Roll out on a floured surface on the counter and knead the air bubbles out. If it seems too sticky, add in a handful of flour and knead until the dough is elastic. If it seems too dry, lay it flat, scoop on a tablespoon more of wild yeast, and work in with your hands, kneading and combining. Seal up in a container or used recycled plastic wrap (for example, the old bags I used to buy bulk oatmeal) and store in the fridge for baking the next day or in the freezer for use after a day. When ready, take out of fridge and allow it to rise to double the size. (If frozen, pull out from freezer and store in fridge overnight before continuing.)

A From the Woods Smoothie

1 cup whole milk vanilla yogurt or plain kefir

Half frozen banana

1/2 cup frozen elderberries

1/4 teaspoon freshly grated ginger

1/4 teaspoon turmeric, fresh or powdered

1 cup chilled Pine Needle Tea with Honey (see page 188)

The secret to blending the perfect smoothie is a soft ingredient to hard ingredient layering system. Wait, is that a secret or does everyone in the world already know that? This foraged smoothie is an amazing way to consume the benefits of pine, which is rich in vitamin A, aiding teeth, bones, soft tissue, white blood cells, the immune system, and mucus membrane health. It has five times the amount of vitamin C found in a lemon, so it's a more efficient way to create goodness inside of you. (See page 188 for how to make your own bulk pine tea.) If you're on the go or headed out for a hike, shake up kefir, pine tea, and turmeric and gulp it down for a quick energy boost.

If you lean on the sweeter side of life, you'll love the vanilla whole milk yogurt added in. But sometimes I just crave more of a tart flavor, so the plain kefir gives it a little kick with less sugar involved. My best friend, Keegan, always shares her new food and beverage discoveries and when we bring our girls together to play, we almost always attempt to fuel each other as moms. "Here, drink this . . . eat this . . . have you had enough water today?" One time she brought a bottle of plain kefir shaken with turmeric powder and a dash of cinnamon, and it was the quickest, most nourishing beverage. It gave me the experience of biting into a tart apple, fresh off the branch at the orchard. It was her inspiration that drew me to the blend of turmeric and plain kefir here.

Add the yogurt to the blender first, followed by the banana, elderberries, ginger, and turmeric, and then flood pine tea on top. Perfection.

Alternate add-ins include chilled powdered spirulina, beet powder, or fresh bee pollen for a gorgeous and delightful from-the-woods nature smoothie.

Forager's Maple Yogurt

1 gallon whole milk

6 to 8 ounces yogurt starter

2 tablespoons vanilla (optional)

2 tablespoons maple syrup (optional), plus more for topping

½ cup raw sugar (optional)

Yogurt was literally a happy accident. It began as a result of milk being stored by primitive methods in warm climates.

Most historical accounts attribute yogurt to the Neolithic peoples of Central Asia around 6000 B.C. Herdsmen began the practice of milking their animals, and the natural enzymes in the carrying containers (animal stomachs) curdled the milk, essentially making yogurt. Not only did the milk then keep longer, it is thought that people preferred the taste so they continued the practice, which then evolved over centuries into commercial yogurt making. Those seem like my kind of people.

"Oh shoot, my milk spoiled and kind of curdled a little bit from the sun. Hmm."

(Strong curiosity sets in . . .)

"I wondering if it might taste good." Tastes it. Loves it. Calls over her lover named Gurt. "Yo! Gurt! You have to taste this!"

And then yogurt came into the world to bless us all.

I don't know if a woman came up with it, but I'd be willing to bet that it was, because, you know, women are amazing.

Sterilize jars or containers for storage by boiling in them in water for about 10 minutes. Let air-dry on a towel.

In a saucepan, slowly heat the whole milk to 185° to 195°F over medium heat. Once it has reached the proper temperature, transfer it into a new pot surrounded by cold water in the sink. Bring the milk down to 120°F. Add in 6 to 8 ounces of yogurt starter. This will bring harvested cultures to the batch. Whisk and finish here, or add vanilla, maple syrup, and/or sugar for a sweeter blend. Whisk evenly!

Funnel the cream into the storage containers or jars and layer maple syrup on top. Seal the jars tightly and then soak in a bath of cold water of about 120°F for about 3 hours. Remove and store in the refrigerator. Yogurt should be creamy and thick!

Bottling up this happy accident has never felt better. You can eat it right out of the jar or top with bee pollen, fresh berries, oats or nuts, or a drizzle of honey.

Bilberry Breakfast Potatoes

1 tablespoon bilberries

Bouquet of cedar tips

2 cups water

4 or 5 burdock roots (these can be foraged or purchased from many co-ops or farmers' markets)

4 medium white potatoes

3 golden beets

4 small sweet potatoes

½ cup butter or coconut oil

Salt and black pepper

NOTE: Starwest Botanicals is a quality bulk-herbs company in the wholesale organic herbs market. As a matter of principle, they only carry the highest quality seeds, powder, or whole herbs. Their huge selection of wholesale organic herbs will have you wondering why you should look any-where else for qual-ity bulk herbs, and yes, they ship worldwide.

Bilberry, or *Vaccinium myrtillus,* is a close relative of the blueberry and is often called huckleberry. The bilberry, also known as blaeberry, whortleberry, or wimberry, is the fruit of a small shrub that grows wild on open acidic land across the British Isles. Bilberry has been sought after for many reasons. Whole dried bilberries have been said to offer many positive uses for promoting eye health. The bilberry leaf and whole bilberry have had many historical uses.

Vaccinium myrtillus taken as a whole dried fruit has been said to have an astringent-like quality. Buying bilberries wholesale in their whole form provides an easy way to take advantage of the great antioxidant properties of this organic herb. It is easy to see the many positive effects that *Vaccinium myrtillus* can produce.

Soak the bilberries for 5 to 10 minutes, then crush them with a mortar and pestle or rock and cutting board. Chop the cedar sprigs down to 1- to 2-inch sections. Boil the cedar tips, nee-dles, and bilberries in the water for 15 minutes—a cast-iron pan is preferred. Set aside and let the cedar steep like a tea.

Wash the burdock root and chop into small edible bites. Peel the white potatoes, if you prefer, although I love the way the skin cooks and adds an earthier texture to this dish. Chop the top and the bottom off the beets' root. Dice into small cubes. Peel the sweet potatoes and chop into small edible squares.

Strain out the cedar tips and bilberries from the water. Cook the burdock root, white and sweet potatoes, and beets in the cast-iron pan in the water until deliciously soft and just perfectly cooked. Add in the butter or coconut oil and let sim-mer and brown and caramelize. Experiment with this. If they are slightly overdone but have increased browning of each potato, they are surprisingly enjoyable as well. The cast-iron pan works each crevice on all sides and heats just right.

Sprinkle salt and pepper on top. For a spiced alternative, sprinkle 1 teaspoon of cumin and 1 teaspoon of cayenne in during the cooking process.

Serve hot. Go fishing.

His Name Was Bilberry Wilbury

He rose with the last glimpse of the moon to harvest his beautiful brown spotted schroom.

Over the rivers, clothed in just slippers. Off to the woods did he go.

But try he did, to search and seek, but no bountiful schroom could he ever quite reach.

They grew so high up on the side of the trunk, and with all that he had he jumped but went splunk.

So, home he journeyed on, at the arrival of dawn, feeling mildly sedated and gloom.

But then not far off, could it be, could it be? A tip-top sprig of a green cedar tree?

He burst and he leapt, shedding all his weighted gloom, to chase as fast as he could for that bloom!

"Climb up! Climb up! Shimmy shimmy!" he cried.

His eyes so big, scanning it 50 feet wide!

He pulled out the brown woven basket with scissors, filled it just full, then leaped back to the rivers.

With rain tenderly falling, his smile oo-ling and ah-ling, he came back from the woods all aglow.

Sprigs and clips and lush cedar tips tossed into the pan with gusto!

He watched it simmer and boil and bubble, rubbed his third day's bushy and most bearded, bristled stubble. Then turned the pan gently down low.

Chop, chop, chop.

Syncing each chop to each fallen raindrop.

Singing ever so sweetly and awfully softly, "Roots, potatoes, berries, and beets. Roots, potatoes, berries, and beets." Then tiptoed in to his love, nestled under the sheets.

"Good morning, my love. Wake up! Wake up! The sun is shining, my small buttercup!"

I have for you, some sweet cedared roots.

And a big round plate of berries, beets, and lush fruits!"

"Oh Bilberry!" She cried. "You've done it once more!" Her smile was bright despite her tiny cold sore.

Then sleepy and softly, they made way to the kitchen, to scoop up some breakfast. Then out they went fishin.

The End.

A Fungi'd Breakfast Bouquet

½ pound spiced ground sausage

About 1 cup each shiitake mushrooms, button mushrooms, morel mushrooms, and chanterelle mushrooms (or any combination of what is in season or available)

2 tablespoons sesame oil

1 red pepper

1 teaspoon salt

1 teaspoon black pepper

4 to 6 sprouted tortillas

Bouquet of raw kale

½ head purple cabbage

4 to 7 sunshine eggs

I sometimes daydream of mini fresh fungi'd bouquets arriving at my front door every Monday. They would be wrapped in linen and dropped off to me by some sort of magical gnome in his red pointy hat who looks up and says, "You've got this. It's going to be a GREAT week!" But when that doesn't happen, I usually make this meal instead.

Mushrooms are incredible sources of fiber, protein, vitamin C, folate, iron, zinc, manganese, vitamin D, thiamine, riboflavin, niacin, vitamin B_6, pantothenic acid, phosphorus, potassium, copper, and selenium. Can you even handle it? It's a lot to take in, literally. I enjoy cooking with sesame oil because it's a lighter oil that spreads evenly onto the mushrooms and leaves a slight hint of nut flavor.

On medium heat, cook the ground spiced sausage until browned.

Chop the mushrooms. This is where believing in your individual preference lies. The mushrooms can be chopped in fine, petite shapes or in chunky, full-bodied ones. I chop them differently based on whom I'm making them for or if I am serving it for a hearty fall morning or a soft spring sunrise. I tend to lean toward the chunky slices because I like to leave a little of the fungi's shape present.

Pour the sesame oil into the pan followed by the fungi'd bouquet. Let them simmer on low to medium heat, flipping occasionally until they eventually reach a lightly browned, slight crispiness on each side. Chop the red pepper and add to the sizzling pan. Sprinkle salt and pepper on top.

Layer on top of a sprouted tortilla and add a fresh bed of springy kale and thinly chopped purple cabbage. Then top with one or two sunshine eggs per tortilla. Super simple and ultimately nourishing. Wrap and fold as if you worked at a floral shop and were about to send a bouquet of fresh flowers out into the world!

Basic Chamomile Oats

5 cups water, whole milk, or vegan milk alternative

3 cups whole rolled oats, plus an extra tablespoon

Fresh bouquet of wild chamomile or 3 tablespoons dried chamomile, plus more flowers for topping

1 tablespoon maple syrup, plus more for topping

NOTE: The liquid to oats ratio is just about 2:1 but I love experimenting with ratios. For a thicker version, stick with the 2:1 ratio but for a smoother, wet bowl, add liquid to make a 3:1 ratio. Begin with your liquid of choice. My favorite choice is cream top whole milk, which makes a most delightful and creamy version of this dish.

Even the most basic of meals can be the most magical. Sometimes I imagine what interactions would be like in the world if everyone was constantly doused in chamomile—if we walked out our doors to air that filled our lungs with peace with each breath. I mean, sign me up for that job as a fairy who flies around dumping baskets of chamomile over scenes of blocked-up traffic and disagreements.

This recipe is a simple staple item to have easily accessible in a giant jar on the counter with the rolled oats and premixed chamomile, just calling your name to be made most mornings. I like oats as a start to the day for the way it actually carries me through the morning with energy and a steady strength. Chamomile grows along fence lines, on roadsides, and in sunny fields from southern Canada to northern United States to western Minnesota and is found at most co-ops in the bulk section. We start so many mornings dripping with a calming bowl of chamomile oats. Wild chamomile can be planted in your back woods, in your raised garden bed, or inside your home in a sunny corner. Folk-focused healing uses chamomile to ward off anxiety, insomnia, menstrual cramps, and headaches, to calm the stomach lining, to help babies with colic, and has even been known to come to the rescue of other sickly plants in a garden when transplanted from the wild. How caring is chamomile?

Slowly bring your liquid of choice to a boil on the stovetop, then turn the heat down to a simmer. Add in the rolled oats and fresh or dried chamomile leaves and flowers, stirring occasionally in between the thoughts mingling in your mind. Simmer for less than 7 minutes—here's where preference comes in. Some like it chunky and thick and others like it smooth and runny. Don't analyze it too much. During the last minute or so of simmering, add in a heaping tablespoon of oats and mix throughout. I love the variation in texture this gives. Top with crushed chamomile flowers and drizzle with maple syrup. Optional add-ons include brown sugar, peanut butter, wild dried blueberries, or chilled milk of choice. Basic. Gorgeous. Nourishing.

Almond Forest Croissants

DOUGH

3 tablespoons unsalted butter

1¾ cups cold whole milk

4 teaspoons instant yeast or 1½ tablespoons wild yeast

3½ cups organic all-purpose unbleached flour

1 cup almond flour

¼ cup raw turbinado sugar

2 teaspoons salt

3 sticks cold butter

FILLING OPTIONS

Dried chamomile

Fresh, frozen elderberries

Dark chocolate

Chopped foraged fungi in season

Raw honey

EGG WASH

1 large egg white

Dash of water

I'm eating a croissant as I write this. The flaky crust is getting all over my keyboard and I'm not even that bothered by it. It feels like a really normal thing to be doing on a Tuesday afternoon. The butter melts into my fingers and the dough sort of sticks to the inside of my mouth as the chocolate and elderberry sink into my belly.

Integrating almond flour and choosing organic, grass-fed butter, raw sugar, and foraged goods for the filling are simple ways to nourish the body. This recipe takes about 2 days to make, so be sure to plan ahead and know it will be well worth the planning and love put into it!

FOR THE DOUGH: The day before you make the croissants, melt the 3 tablespoons of butter with the whole milk gently on the stove over a low heat. Whisk in the yeast. Pour into your mixer and add in the flours, sugar, and salt. Beat on a low until the dough has a chance to combine all together and then turn up to medium for a few minutes until the dough is combined and slightly sticky. Pull the dough out of the mixer, place onto parchment paper, and gently roll to form a rectangle about 10 inches by 7 inches and about 1 inch thick. Wrap in recycled plastic or an old, clean reusable bag. (Collect and save your bags from your bulk section finds and store these away to pull from for plastics, if able.) Refrigerate for 1 hour.

Slice the sticks of butter into halves, the long way. Lay out the butter to form a square, with each half stick resting up against the next and imagine how it will sit right on top of your rectangular dough in the refrigerator. Lay a piece of parchment paper on top of your butter and beat it ever so gently. Now really get in there and pound it good, keeping it in the square formation. Refrigerate for 30 minutes.

Daydream of the fluffy forest croissant.

Take the dough out of the refrigerator and lay it on a floured surface on the counter. Then take out the square of butter and place it in the center of the rectangle. Fold the ends in and then

recipe continues

The Round Bellied Baker

I learned how to make croissants when I worked as a baker in a small town cafe when the Bear and I were first married. It wasn't far from our first apartment, which had French floral wallpaper, rose floral carpet, a big clawfoot bathtub, and creaky, smelly stairs that led up to our abode. Oh, to be back there in my mind is a joy. We would lie in bed, tucked under the sheets, and hear music out the window from the downtown river festivities.

We spent summer evenings walking through the streets, dreaming of homes and our future together. Awaking each morning at 3:45 am, I would kiss my Bear goodbye and walk my round, pregnant belly up a few blocks to the bakery in the town. Sometimes I would ride my bike there, too, and I am certain that I didn't value those moonlit morning bike rides quite enough. I opened up the shop in the dark, turned on the lights and music, and tied my apron tight over my growing uterus. I started with the baguettes for the day and prepared the morning blueberry and cranberry scones, croissants, and breads of the day. It alternated between cranberry, whole wheat, and the most delightful olive bread I've ever tasted. I worked there up until I was so round I could hardly lean into the mixer to scrape out the bread dough. I remember days when I felt so tired and sweaty, rolling out chocolate croissants and growing a life at same time, but the work was a joy. I learned so much about baking, and I learned so much about myself. Being alone in the early mornings, peeking to check on both the sun and bread rising almost simultaneously, was one of the most rewarding jobs I've ever had. I am so thankful. I learned many skills from an incredibly knowledgeable baker who showed me everything by hand, the way I learn best. I spent evenings in the apartment with Max, researching and studying the recipes. I made mistakes but to this day, if I close my eyes and think hard enough, I can almost smell it all and remember the look on Max's face when I brought home fresh scones and butter croissants that I had made that morning. Bears love scones and round-bellied foxes. What a joy and what a memory. When I make croissants for my three girls now and the mess is substantial, I can't help but reflect back to life before them. Then to have them devouring buttered delights along with me makes me smile even more. Flour and butter everywhere!

NOTE: Fridge and freezer space is needed for this preparation: If you're anything like me and they're always jam-packed with goods, prepare to move things around a bit to make room for the in and out, in and out of this recipe.

rotate 90 degrees to have it elongated up and down in front of you. Combine in the butter. Roll out, fold in thirds. Roll out, fold in thirds. Do this three or four times until the butter is fully combined. The final roll will be 24 inches by 8 inches in a rectangular shape. End by folding into thirds. Refrigerate for 2 hours. Go on a walk. Breathe. Enjoy the details and time that this recipe requires. (Or take a nap and fuel up for your next hike.)

Back with intention, take out the dough and roll it into an 18- by 16-inch rectangle with the short ends on the side. At the base of the rectangle dough, start to cut short slices about 3 inches apart. Make mountains with your cuts—long steep triangles that reach toward the top of the dough and then back down. The number of croissants will determined by how narrow or wide your cuts are, so imagine and anticipate whether you want mini ones or big, buttery ones.

Ever so gently, pull the triangles apart to stretch just slightly. Be sure that each triangle has a small slit at the base of the wide portion. Fill them at the wide base with small handfuls of dried chamomile, fresh, frozen, or foraged elderberries, wild mushrooms, or dark chocolate. Then roll them up, starting at the wide base, tucking in the fillings, and ending with the point. Gently pull the "peak" of the mountain, or the top of the triangle, to hug the rest of the croissant. Bring the two ends to curve around like a "C" and place on a sheet pan lined with parchment paper. Continue to roll each of them. Cover in plastic wrap or saved up recycled bags or materials. Refrigerate overnight.

Good morning! Preheat the oven to 400°F. Take the croissants out of the refrigerator and let rise to double their size.

FOR THE EGG WASH: Crack open an egg and let just the white escape into a bowl. Save the yoke, if you can, for tomorrow morning's scrambled eggs. Combine the egg white with a dash of water and whisk with a fork to combine. Brush the liquid just slightly on top of each of the croissants.

Bake for 12 minutes. Turn the pan around in the oven about halfway through.

So much effort for that first bite of plush, flakey, buttery croissant, which will feel like such an accomplishment.

NOTE: During fall and winter months, add in a dash of cloves, pumpkin spice seasoning, or nutmeg for some warmth and depth. For spring and summer, add in a dash of fresh thyme or lemon seasoning for a burst of light goodness.

Floraled Elderflower Quiche

CRUST

1 cup quinoa

2 cups water
(or other liquid)

¼ cup softened butter

1 large egg

1 teaspoon cinnamon

FILLING

5 chicken eggs or
4 duck eggs

Splash of organic
whole milk or cream

2 tablespoons butter,
room temperature

A few sprigs of fresh
rosemary

½ cup black olives

About ¼ cup shiitake
mushrooms

Black activated charcoal
salt or smoked salt

Breakfast sausage,
cooked bacon, or a dash
of maple syrup (optional)

2 tablespoons calendula
floral petals

1 cup foraged elderflowers

A most feminine and floraled quiche. A go-to for bridal or baby showers, birthday parties, morning tea, Sunday breakfast, or to impress your mother-in-law with.

FOR THE CRUST: To make the quinoa, use a ratio of 1 cup uncooked quinoa to 2 cups liquid. Bring the quinoa and liquid to a boil in a medium saucepan. Reduce heat to low, cover and simmer until tender and most of the liquid has been absorbed, 15 to 20 minutes. Fluff with a fork.

Preheat the oven to 375°F.

Mix in the butter, egg, and cinnamon. Lay out flat on the bottom of a pie pan. Press down tenderly and build up the side of the crust to connect to the side of the pan. Bake in the oven for 10 to 15 minutes until golden brown. Cool.

FOR THE FILLING: Turn the oven down to 350°F. Put the eggs, whole milk or cream, and butter into a bowl and whisk. Peel the leaves from the stem of the rosemary and chop finely. Cut the black olives into small Os and set aside. Brush any dirt off the mushrooms and barely rinse them in water. If the stems are tender enough, you can use the entire portion but if not, remove the bases of the mushrooms and only use the caps. Slice the shiitakes into small edible portions. Combine the mushrooms, rosemary, olives, and salt in the bowl with the egg mixture and whisk together. Pour into the cooled crust. If you're opting for meat, chop in small edible pieces and sprinkle throughout. Add a dash of maple syrup, if you wish. You can experiment with baking in the calendula floral petals or top the quiche with them after baking. Bake for 30 to 40 minutes.

Garnish with the elderflowers or other fresh edible flowers. Seek edible floral petals in each season! Here are a few substitutes.

Chamomile	Hibiscus	Jasmine	Poppy
Chrysanthemum	Hollyhock	Lavender	Red clover
Dandelion	Honeysuckle	Mallow	Wood sorrel

Charcoal and Beet Toast

2 slices sprouted bread

3 tablespoons butter or goat cheese

½ tablespoon charcoal powder or beet powder

In case you don't have time for a 67-step croissant, but want to start the day with something nourishing and magical, this is your ticket. Charcoal powder and beet powder both offer absolutely incredible nourishment. The beets add to your system, with vitamins, minerals, energy, and a sustaining texture of slight sweetened earth. The charcoal powder essentially takes away or draws out from within. Depending on what you need, each of these can provide that. If you wake up feeling bloated or had too much wine the night before, the charcoal powder may help cleanse your gut and when paired with much water, may aid in that bloated feeling. The beet powder will help you start your day with a burst of energy and nutrients. As always, discuss with your open-minded doctor regarding your specific health and nutritional needs. The charcoal powder can interact with certain medications, so be sure to explore your own journey with this. The following is a single serve combination. For more, feel free to double or triple the ingredients to your liking.

Toast the slices of bread just slightly. Stroke on room-temperature butter or chilled goat cheese. Sprinkle with charcoal powder or beet powder. Fold in half or devour as an open-faced delight.

OTHER USES FOR ACTIVATED CHARCOAL POWDER

- Cleanses and whitens teeth
- Alleviates gas and bloating
- Treats alcohol poisoning or a hangover
- Removes digestive toxins
- Treats acne, bee, snake, mosquito bites when mixed with coconut oil
- Cleanses body and brain of toxins, eliminates "brain fog," and thus is anti-aging
- May prevent the onset of the flu or other stomach bacteria by trapping them and carrying them out safely

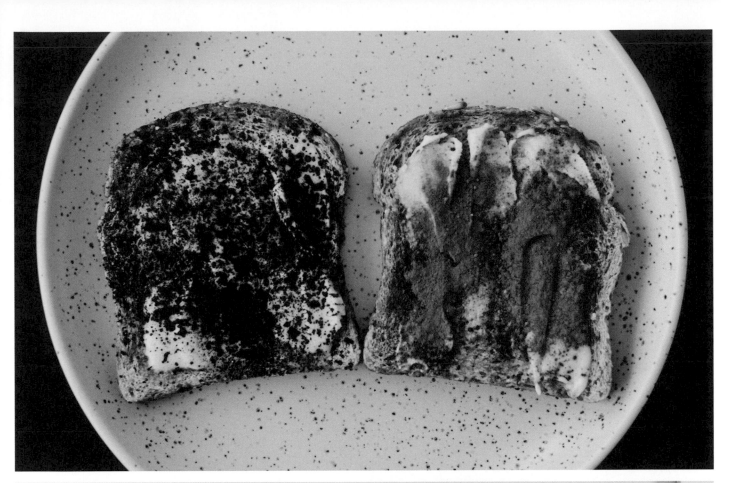

ACV Honey Scramble

¹⁄₄ stick grass-fed butter

4 or 5 eggs

2 tablespoons apple cider vinegar and honey blend "with the mother" (Bragg Organic Apple Cider Vinegar and Honey Blend)

We went for a long family hike in the backyard woods this morning. It was so amazing how good the cold air felt on our cheeks as we explored new corners of the woods, and everything seemed alive and animate. We appreciated new trees we had never seen before and felt unbelievably grateful to live where we were. Isn't it a wonder, just how quickly discontentment may set in? Something we viewed with such delight can so quickly turn to be underappreciated or devalued. If only we could trap that feeling of being full of gratitude and a thankfulness to even be alive. I wish I could start every morning with this perspective. We came indoors from our hike and prepared eggs with organic unfiltered apple cider vinegar with honey. It contains "the mother," which contains strands of proteins, enzymes, and alimentative bacteria. It aids in digestion, boosts energy, and is a small addition that makes a huge difference to simple morning eggs! The simplistic form of this offering reminds me to get back to the essence of all that is good. Transcend to curiosity and taste. And butter.

In a large low skillet, melt the butter over medium heat. Crack the eggs into the melted butter, add the apple cider vinegar with honey, and whisk. Leave the eggs just slightly wet. Turn off stove and let them finish cooking from the heat of the pan. Flip one more time evenly as you prepare the forks and plates.

Minnesota Wild Rice
French Toast

2 cups wild rice

4 eggs

1 tablespoon cinnamon,
plus more to sprinkle

¼ teaspoon cloves

¼ teaspoon ginger

½ cup honey

Dash of cream or
whole milk

Half loaf of sprouted
bread

½ stick butter, room
temperature

Baking wild rice French toast is like baking up the Midwest. Drizzling it with warmed maple syrup fresh from the trees, grass-fed butter, and a sprinkling of fresh cinnamon makes for the perfect Saturday morning feast! The thing I love about this recipe is that it's perfect for serving friends or family when hosting them for breakfast. All the French toast is hot and ready at the same time instead of making slices individually and having to reheat or attempt to keep them warm in the corner of the stovetop. It's such a beautiful dish to serve with dripping maple syrup or peanut butter stroked on top.

Soak the wild rice in water while you prepare the rest of the ingredients.

Preheat the oven to 375°F. Prepare a loaf pan by buttering the sides and bottom.

In a bowl, mix the eggs, cinnamon, cloves, ginger, and honey. Whisk together with a dash of cream or whole milk! Take about half of the wild rice and layer on the bottom of the loaf pan. Dip the sprouted bread pieces in the egg mixture, one at a time, and immerse them completely in the wet ingredients. Embrace the mess. Swing each piece of bread over from the wet bowl to the pan, lining them all up, one by one, to stand straight up in a row. Pinch off sections of butter and line them up on top of the soaked bread. Sprinkle the rest of the wild rice on top and add a dash of cinnamon. Cover with baking parchment paper or a flat pan (to save paper product use).

Bake for 28 to 30 minutes, then uncover and bake for an additional 10 minutes until browned. The result will be a soft, moist version of French toast. If you prefer the traditional French toast experience with all the crispy goodness, lay the pieces of soaked bread flat out on a sheet pan, and turn halfway through baking, letting both sides be thoroughly baked.

Wild Rice Minnesota Th...
Sprouted Bread
2 cups wild Rice
cinnamon
cloves
ginger
1/2 cup Tu...
1/2 stick
2 egg

Forest nurse log (n).

A large fallen tree on which other trees and plants sprout as the wood decays, with the roots of the seedlings often straddling the log as they reach down to the soil; some burst directly from the fallen log. The large log aids with its own dead body. A seed from a tree close by can also land on the log, and if it's able to receive sufficient light, it can germinate. The bark holds in moisture like a sponge for the young plant. As the seedling sprouts, it shoots the roots down to the ground and gains strength to thicken. Fungi joins in and feasts on the dead log's wood, as slowly it rots and in turn provides suste-nance to the growing buds for years to come.

The Tree Named Fern

A STUDY ON "NURSE LOGS" IN THE FOREST

There once was a tree named Fern. She was strong, brave, and the kindest tree in the forest. Her trunk was wildly round and provoked the earthiest shade of cocoa. Her inner sap dripped of caramel gold. She was delightful. She was magical. She grew up high to the sky, as high as the eye could see.

Most mornings, the birds of the forest came to sing a tune, then through the afternoon they rested their tired, small wings on her long branches. Fern had lived in the forest for many years and although her spirit was young, her bark showed many signs of age. She gave and she gave and she gave to those who needed her. One day as the forest grew dark, a big storm started brewing into the air. The trees seemed to talk to each other and comfort one another in times like this. Fern tried to stand strong in the pouring rain and wind but it was a mighty wind, a passionate wind. She felt her roots loosen in the ground from all the rain. She was worn and tired and she knew her time in the forest was drawing near to the end. So with one last mighty stretch up to the sky, she lifted her roots from the ground and her highest branches up to the clouds and fell to her side, gently back to lie on the earth as if it were her bed. The storm slowed. The forest grew quiet. The birds flew from their nests to come see her, as a light gray mist almost filled the sky around dear old Fern. There was a sadness that filled the corners of the forest, and every tree seemed to curve in a little toward her that night. But then, as morning came the very next day, as mornings always do, a small and curious little squirrel came bounding through the forest.

He was new in the area, so his eyes were wide with wonder as he hopped and jumped from this moss-covered log to that moss-covered log. He was beaming with excitement, until suddenly, he paused and looked down to find he was standing on top of Fern's giant tree trunk, which rested peacefully there on its side as if it were already tenderly sinking into the earth. Observant as it was, the squirrel immediately noticed a very small green sprout. It was as small as a mushroom and a wildly bright shade of green. The squirrel jumped over it and noticed another and another and another. It began to grow right in front of the squirrel's eyes. Dancing toward the sky, becoming taller and taller, shooting right up toward the clouds, coming directly out of Fern's old worn and wrinkly tree trunk. Fern began to burst new trees from herself that began to grow, and grow, and GROW until one day they reached the sky. That same, kind tree, the kindest tree in all the land, kept on giving and giving and giving everything she had until one day there were 17 new trees that had grown up to the clouds from Fern. Kindness filled the forest again. Little children came to sit on Fern, like a most magical bench in the woods. The birds visited her branches once more and the forest was filled with a song of hope again.

Catching Wild Yeast

2 cups flour (organic unbleached white flour works well)

2 cups nonchlorinated filtered water

There is yeast floating in soil, on plants, even in the air all around us, and some of this yeast will make its way to your flour and water mixture. Foraging for yeast is wildly rewarding, simple, and magical. Yeast will begin to grow and divide almost immediately, and you'll experience the process around 48 hours later and fall in love. The froth is caused by the carbon dioxide that the yeast builds up and creates. The starter will also have *Lactobacillus,* a good bacteria, in it. This lends the slightly acidic flavor to the bread by creating lactic acid, which you will see form in the bubbles as well as notice when the smell increases. It will be bready, and yeasty, with hints of fermented alcohol. It craves to be fed every other day and can be refrigerated if you'd like to slow the growth down for feeding every 5 or 6 days. I love this process because it reminds me about what life was like for women and men baking bread before "active yeast powder" was invented in 1859.

In a large glass or clay jar, mix the flour and the water. Gently mix to combine. Notice bubbles forming and the fermentation process beginning. Cover with cheesecloth and tie with string or a rubber band. Store away from direct light. Care for every other day, by gently stirring and adding equal parts flour and water.

1   2   3

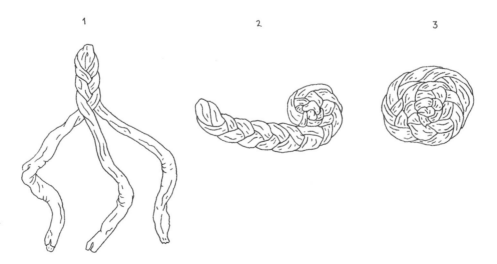

Parenting like a Forager

I've always been obsessed with the idea of wilderness living and wilderness parenting. Not listening to what society has set up for us or deemed as "acceptable" or "not acceptable," not blindly obeying what baby books or baby blogs say or what other lifestyle mom bloggers do, but staring into the heart of a child and making a decision based on that alone. What will nourish this child the most, apart from the supposed-tos and rules? How can I use my hands and heart in the greatest possible way to mold and shape this child, even if it's not the most efficient route? How can I wake up every single day and be open-minded to the challenges and the mishaps and the spills and the emotions? I want to look around with fresh eyes without expectations for what I will find or expectations for how the outer world will interact with me, but rather with a genuine open-minded approach toward viewing their tiny small worlds with importance and care and tenderness.

I also channel this idea into my bread. Traveling back into time when there were no stand mixers and bread thermometers, there were just two hands, ingredients, a heating source, and intuition. A survivalist in the woods could turn cattail roots into flour, mix flour with fresh warmed water and yeast from the preparation ahead of time and bake. Wild yeast is rewarding to care for and beyond simple and intriguing. Starting from nothing, home-grown yeast makes a most curious combination and essential ingredient to a forager's bread.

Snow Honey Loaf

One morning, as the snow fell heavily outside, I awoke with an intense craving for homemade bread. The snow fell almost in sheets of white with the biggest flakes drifting tenderly toward the earth. I laid on my pillow staring at it fall out the window. It was cleansing the earth, yet here all I could do was think of warm bread. I had to have it and I had to have it right then.

The light poured into the window gently and for a brief second, I recalled what it felt like to sleep in, pre-babies. A sleep-in after having children will never be the same. Before babies, one could stay locked together in bed, cancel plans, and tuck warm body to warm body without disruption. The silence would have filled the room instead of a white noise sound machine. The bed would seemingly go on for miles and miles in comfort and peace. But mornings with little lives are fun, too. There are the tender, high-pitched voices that exude opinions and thoughts, and I mean high-pitched in a good way, like sweet little soft babylike voices. There's someone who needs you. Someone wants you to care for them and there's the hope of a brand new day. Mornings with children are beautiful, too.

So, anyway, this one fine morning, I awoke with the sensation and desire for buttery bread. Plush, warm baked bread, where the butter just drips right off and melts all over the plate and you wipe it clean with the last bite of a bread slice. I awoke, put clothes on, went into the kitchen with a small hand in each of mine, and then 2 hours later, my husband was gone with the car and I had completely forgotten about my longing for fresh baked bread. That's the thing with little lives—one could have the strongest desire for something and yet it dissipates so quickly, without even blinking an eye, because the little lives matter more. The girls settled into coloring, as they do most mornings, and I remembered my craving for homemade bread. So I went into the kitchen to prepare it. I pulled the ingredients from the shelves. Flour, honey, wild yeast, raw cane sugar, cardamom, salt, water. Wait, where's the water? We weren't able to drink the water at the A-frame when we first moved in, so we got into the habit of buying filtered water from our co-op and nourishing ourselves with it instead until we got the well fixed. But today, there was no water left. The Bear had the car and there I was, absolutely needing a loaf of warm bread in my life. I looked under the cabinet by the coffee where we store it, but nothing. I looked in the back stock water area over by the stairs. Nothing. I even looked in the backup to the backup area underneath the kitchen island and thought I spotted one, but it was empty. I sat staring out the window until the solution was obvious. The snow! Of course, the snow. It's what any pioneer would've done years and winters ago. Wouldn't they collect from a river in the spring and summer and melt the snow in the winter? It was worth a try. So, I put on my boots, the same boots that send off a metaphoric alarm to the girls that says, "MOM IS GOING OUTSIDE." They broke from their coloring and shot toward the door wearing a cloth diaper and zipped-up footie pajamas and started making noises like a small herd. So 15 minutes later, we were all bundled and went outside with nothing but open eyes and a large copper pot. The girls helped me collect. It was snowing so hard, it was as if the snow filled the pot itself in the same amount of time it took us three to ball up handfuls of snow and pour into the pot. I think we were slower mostly because both of the girls stuffed handfuls into their mouth with each gathered grab. But finally, the pot was overflowing. It sat on the ground for awhile and extra flakes layered on top while we continued to play in the woods. I love the way my 1-year-old just shook her head, "no," when I ask her if she wants to go back inside. She has quite literally said "no" every time I have asked her. My 4½-year-old could be convinced with hot cocoa or books on the couch, but no . . . .not my Minoux. So eventually she followed us back inside and our copper pot of snow came along. We stripped back down to our warm cozies and squeezed each other's hands to exchange warmth. We hung our wool on the drying rack and turned on the Carpenters' record, which Luella is "just really into lately," and the sound filled the home.

I put the pot on the stove and warmed it up, checking back to see it melting slowly. I combined the salt and flour and a dash of sugar. The water was just warm, so I scooped it out in a measuring cup and added it to the yeast, the cardamom, and the dash of maple syrup that I sometimes add to breads. I mixed the ingre-

dients. It was a little on the sticky and wet side, so I gently added a handful of flour to the mix and continued combining. I wiped my dirty hands on my apron, took another handful of flour and sprinkled it onto the counter in a circular fashion. I reached into the bowl to scoop out the dough, scraping and almost tapping at it, to release from the sides of the bowl. I alternated the dough in each hand back and forth, back and forth, before plopping down onto the floured counter. I enveloped the dough in my hands, making an O-shaped grasp, like an embrace and then starting the knead—pushing out to my window that overlooked the woods, then flipping the dough back toward me and repeating this, over and over and over. Kneading bread is a sort of heavenly experience, if no one is tugging at your apron. Even on days when my littlest is playing with flour and it's all over my kitchen floor, just to hear her curiosity with that substance while I knead is the simplest joy for me as her mother. I chopped up fresh rosemary with my herb cutter and sprinkled it into the center of the dough to be tucked in.

I let the bread rise with a parchment paper on top. It took about 4 hours to rise to double the size. Time always goes fast when mothering, and I nearly forgot about the bread again, but the mess was there to remind me. I put it in the oven at 350°F for 40 minutes and pulled it out to see the top layer of dough browning every so slightly. Bread always finishes cooking from within, so I set it on the stove to complete its course and waited 20 more minutes. I picked it up, tucked it in my linen apron, and set it on my wooden cutting board next to my brass plate of butter that was premade, sprinkled with black pepper, and ready to be spread, of course. I went to the table with nothing else but my butter and a knife and the bread. The girls came running as they do when I sit down, and we sat and ate warm bread together. The butter dripped all over my plate and I was obligated to swoop it up clean with the last piece of cut loaf. It was perfect.

4 cups freshly fallen snow (2 cups boiling water)

1½ cups oats (plus ½ cup for sprinkling)

¼ cup maple syrup

2 tablespoons honey

¼ cup butter

1 tablespoon instant yeast or 2½ tablespoons wild yeast

2½ cups whole wheat flour

2 cups unbleached all purpose flour or ivory flour

Pinch of salt

Olive oil for greasing

Forage freshly fallen snow. Bring indoors and heat over medium heat until it comes to a roaring boil for at least 5 minutes. Strain and sift any leaves, pines needles, or debris. Let cool for about 10 minutes. Mix together the oats, maple syrup, snow water, honey, and butter. Add the yeast in slowly while stirring gently. Add the flour in slowly while mixing on low in a mixer until combined. The dough should be slightly sticky but smooth. Mix in alternate variations below, if desired. Knead gently with hands, then transfer to a big greased pan and cover with a damp towel to rise for 1 hour. Cut in half to freeze 1 portion for later, serve as 2 loaves or keep to bake as 1 large loaf! Place in slightly greased loaf or round pan and let rise for another hour. Sprinkle on top with oats, spices, or chopped herbs. Bake at 350 degrees for 40 minutes in a round bread pan or covered on a sheet pan. Remove covering for the last few minutes. Take out and let cool for 20 minutes before serving.

*Alternate variations include: pinch of cinnamon, cloves, black pepper, beet powder, black charcoal (no more than 1 tablespoon), freshly chopped rosemary, oregano, sage, edible foraged flower petals, finely chopped foraged mushrooms, or powdered mushroom of choice.

Serve with a side of honey or take any of the alternate variations to mix in with butter and watch the snow fall!

Chapter 3
LUNCH

Sunflower and Rose Jelly Sandwich

ROSE CONFECTION-
JAM-SYRUP

3 cups water

4 cups raw sugar

6 to 8 cups rose petals

1 to 2 tablespoons lemon juice (optional)

SUNFLOWER SEED
BUTTER

2 cups sunflower seeds

¼ cup sunflower oil

Sprouted bread

My midwife gifted us with the sweetest, most magical rose confection after she helped bring our youngest daughter into the world. She introduced me to the utilization of bush roses without fertilizer or anything. The amount of petals depends on what outcome is desired—whether confection, jam, or syrup. You can't do it wrong, other than choosing nonchemically sprayed roses. The measurements are very adjustable. When the rosebuds are on the verge of opening, she says that she tells them how lovely they are with great expectation. She always lets them have that day to fulfill their purpose. Using no scissors or blade, she removes the white base of the petals to avoid bitterness. She let their goodness fill her senses—the aroma, velvety softness in her hand, and occasional thorn prick. It all adds up to the feeling of a satisfying cooperation. Talking to them all the while, she lays the petals in her basket. For those that fall by the wayside or are damaged for some reason, she thanks them for doing all they could. She says, "It is the same way I hope I treat people. Then into the kitchen I go." I couldn't agree more.

FOR THE SYRUP: Heat the water and sugar until the sugar is well dissolved. Then add 6 to 8 cups of rose petals. To measure the rose petals, let them slip lightly into a cup, but do not pack them. Let this mixture simmer for ½ to 1 hour, stirring often. At first it will look like way too many petals, but they cook down. Add more water if needed—petals vary in moisture. Lemon juice is optional but adding it helps their color and adds a bit of excitement to the flavor.

The syrup can be put in jars at whatever stage you desire and used fresh or it can be canned (in a 10-minute water bath). Gift away or store for your family.

FOR THE SUNFLOWER BUTTER: Blend the seeds and oil in a blender or food processor until creamy.

Spread the syrup and sunflower butter on two slices of bread for each person.

Foraged Mushroom
French Fries

5 cups chopped in-season foraged mushrooms (chanterelles are my favorite)

10 medium-size Yukon gold potatoes (white center)

1 cup sunflower or olive oil

½ cup organic sumac powder

Salt and black pepper

Bouquet of fresh rosemary

Heirloom Homemade Ketchup (see page 232) or Sumac Lime Dip (see page 234)

The deep red berries of edible sumac burst life onto these french fries and add the perfect amount of tangy, lemon taste and pop of color and wonder. There are many kinds of sumac that are native to an ample number of regions ranging from the East Coast, all the way through the Midwest, the South, and upper northern regions as well. Poison sumac has ivory white berries and is generally found in partly wooded swamps. The dwarf sumac has a velvety leaf and twig combination. They are found in fields and uplands. The smooth and staghorn sumacs have red-toned berries and hairless stems. They are generally found in fields, between old fences, and in state parks and wooded county areas. They prefer partial shade to sunny and semi-dry woodland edges, savannas, prairies, outcrops, road-sides, railroads, and some shores. They bloom June through July and can be harvested through fall. Smooth sumac ranges anywhere from 3 to 18 feet tall and its bigger sister plant, the staghorn sumac, can grow as tall as 35 feet!

The bristly red hair that covers the head of the seeds is filled with ascorbic acid, making it easily rendered into a most refreshing, bright red summertime beverage! Seek out specific harvesting guidelines for your region. It is more common these days for co-ops and specialty grocery stores to carry sumac powder, and it makes an excellent addition for a dash of zing to the plate!

Chop the mushrooms into long strips to mirror the shape of a traditional french fry.

Wash the potatoes under cold water. Peel them or leave the skin on. Preference is key here! I prefer to leave the skin on. Slice the potato in half the long way first, then flip the freshly cut side down on the cutting board, and slice each half the long

recipe continues

way once again so you will have four pieces of potato. Begin on one side and slice the potato in long strips to the girth of your liking. Some afternoons call for big, chunky fries, where double dipping is a must and the fries become a main dish—not as a side. On other days or for serving to kids, the potatoes seem to crave being sliced in thin petite strips. So delicate and magical and almost springy-like! An alternate form of slicing is to use a food processor to make coins or use a mandoline slicer to form the fries into ribbonlike glory.

Preheat the oven to 450°F.

In a bowl, combine the mushrooms, potatoes, olive oil, sumac powder, salt, and pepper. Mix evenly. Lay parchment paper down on your biggest sheet pan and pour the contents of the bowl onto the paper. Spread evenly with your hands and line up the mushrooms and potatoes so that they do not layer on top of one another. Bake for 25 to 28 minutes, turning once about halfway though, until golden brown and the potato is soft to the fork.

While the potatoes and mushrooms bake, gently peel the leaves of the rosemary away from the stem. Chop finely. Sprinkle the fresh rosemary on top of the fries immediately after pulling them out from the oven, so the heat draws out their flavor and they have a chance to "stick" to the fries. Some of the sumac and rosemary will be left behind on the tray, so be open to using a fork or spoon to scoop them up and sprinkle them on top of each dollop of homemade ketchup or dip!

Serve with a cold afternoon beer or chilled sparkling water!

Turmeric Meadowsweet Soup

1 bag carrots (about
1 pound)

Handful of fresh
asparagus

4 medium-size potatoes,
unpeeled

1 cup chopped mushrooms
(in season)

1 cup sunflower oil

2 cups water

1 cup jasmine rice

6 cups water or fresh
maple sap

5 or 6 stems thyme, plus
a bouquet for topping

4 tablespoons turmeric
powder or 3 small
turmeric roots, plus
more for topping

2 tablespoons ginger
powder or 1 small
ginger root

1 cup English peas

Traditional Medicinals'
Turmeric with
Meadowsweet &
Ginger tea

Honey or dash of
maple syrup

Turmeric's wide appeal may have recently gained momentum here in the West, but this healing root has been celebrated as a cooking spice, dye, and medicinal herb in India for more than 3,000 years. Used in Ayurveda and Traditional Chinese Medicine to support everything from digestion and the respiratory system to everyday discomfort and depression, it has such an enduring legacy.

The goal of this soup is a soft, welcoming texture and aroma. This soup pairs well with the season, warm and rich and thick like a stew in winter, and then once the warmer days are here, I keep the soup more free-flowing and lighter in texture. The turmeric bubbles up on the top of the pot as it cooks and is utterly rich and foamy and delightful both in flavor and color. The palette captures the essence of the most intense sunset. Such a deep yellow, it almost as if a pastel drawing crayon was crushed and molded into an edible. It pairs well with a warm or iced glass of Traditional Medicinals' Turmeric with Meadowsweet & Ginger tea.

First, chop the carrots, asparagus, and potatoes into small pieces. In the fall and winter, I make my cuts chunkier and wider. In the spring and summer, I chop them skinnier and lighter. Put the chopped vegetables, mushrooms, and sunflower oil into a pot and simmer on medium for about 5 minutes, stirring here and there. This allows the oil to soak into the vegetables but they don't get overly caramelized or burned.

In a separate pan, bring 2 cups of water to a boil and pour in the jasmine rice. Turn to simmer over a medium heat and cover. The rice will cook for about 20 minutes, or until all the water has left your sight when you peek into the pot. Set aside, uncovered, so the rice does not oversteam. Jasmine rice makes for a tender bite with each spoonful, fueling the belly with warmth and fullness.

recipe continues

NOTE: English peas
are known as shell
peas or garden
peas. They grow
inside the same
home as snap peas
and enjoy a short-
lived season during
late spring and
early summer.
They are harvested
at their best in May.

Pour the water or sap, if available, into the pot with the vegetables.

Place four fingers on the top of the thyme stem and gracefully pull down to separate the leaves from the stem. Chop these leaves finely and toss into the pot. Add in the turmeric and ginger. If you are using fresh roots of each, chop finely, as small as possible to simmer into the base of the soup.

Let vegetables simmer on low to medium heat for about 25 minutes.

Don't forget your peas! These are my favorite! Their firm pop and fresh flavor adds so much texture and excitement. Once the soup has simmered for 25 minutes, sneak out a carrot or potato and blow to cool it down, then test its softness. If it feels just about right, add in the rice and peas and simmer for another 5 minutes. Sometimes I drizzle a little extra sunflower oil in on top and swoosh it all around together.

Tie a small amount of baker's twine around the bundle of thyme for presentation. It can hang on the side of the pot, dipping in just tenderly like a tea bag, presented on the side of the final bowl, or chopped finely and kneaded into butter for warm bread. Sprinkle some chopped fresh turmeric root or turmeric powder on top of the soup or bread. The tea can be made ahead of time in bulk to be warmed or served as a cold beverage on the side, slightly sweetened with honey or a dash of maple syrup!

NOTE: Traditional Medicinals' Turmeric with Meadowsweet & Ginger tea is reinforced with meadowsweet—historically used in traditional European herbal medicine much like turmeric is in Ayurveda—and the warming properties of ginger. Their innovative formula supports a healthy response to inflammation associated with exercise, while also promoting healthy digestion. The team at Traditional Medicinals goes to great lengths to make sure their products do what they say they are going to do. This process starts with the formulation, carries through into responsible sourcing, and ends in their laboratory to confirm what they have worked hard to achieve. I would choose them over any other brand for their intense connection to the sustainability and care they offer throughout the entire start-to-finish process.

Forest Burgers

1 pound ground turkey

Himalayan salt block

1 bunch flowering chives

2 cups chopped button or shiitake mushrooms

1 stem fresh peppermint (long enough to make ¼ teaspoon chopped)

1 stem fresh rosemary

Olive oil

4 ounces honey goat cheese

Bouquet of rainbow radishes

4 whole wheat sprouted hamburger buns

Spicy Homemade Mustard (see page 83)

1 cup live micro greens or sprouts

1 heirloom tomato

1 tablespoon poppy seeds

Imagine a burger bursting with blooming fungi and flowering chives that simply drips of the woods! The blooms drop and pop out the side of the burger. Imagine! This is the ultimate forest burger, capturing all the elements of the forest floor—the tall trees in whole wheat color, live micro greens exuding the texture and the essence of fresh brightened green moss, the wild shiitake mushrooms that grow beneath the trees, and red fresh red tomatoes symbolizing the magical red and white spotted fungi. The sprinkled poppy seeds are the blue jays of the woods. The bites of erupting creamy cheese are moist as the clouds, and the bare hint of peppermint is like a breath of fresh woodland air!

This makes about four decent-size patties but be open to the magic of mini and try cooking smaller ones. Or double the recipe for big burly forest burgers! Just dig in and explore! They can be grilled, baked, simmered over an open fire, or cooked directly in a pan on the stove.

Begin by pulling the meat out of the fridge to soften up. Be sure it's not frozen.

Stack two stove grates on top of one another and place the himalayan salt block on top. Turn the heat on low to warm it ever so slowly.

Begin by chopping. Explore here: I am drawn to large chunks of chives and fungi dripping out, but depending on whom you're serving, they might need to be cut into smaller, more edible bites. Try both and decide which you are drawn to! Chop the flowered chives. Slice half of the mushrooms into small chunks and set the other half aside for later. Peel the leaves of peppermint and rosemary off the stem and chop into teeny small sections using an herb chopper or sharp knife.

In a bowl, combine the ground turkey, chives, mushrooms, peppermint, rosemary, and a splash of olive oil. Squish and mix with your hands. Get it all in there and combine until even. Pinch off small sections of the honey goat cheese about the size of a pea and gently fold into the turkey mix. Form into round patties.

recipe continues

HELLO, MY NAME IS HELGA

There once was a tiny red mushroom named Helga. She was so red, redder than the reddest ripe strawberry. She was so small that no one ever heard her. Every day she wanted to be seen and heard, but all the other mushrooms in Mushroom Land were much bigger and smarter and had much busier things to do besides listening to such a small mushroom. You see, Mushroom Land was a place where what you DID mattered. There were mushroom goals and agendas, places to be and people to see. Life moved so fast. The things Helga cared about seemed different than what the other mushrooms cared about. She cared about the color of the sky and the way the breeze felt on her teeny tiny cap. She wondered how many birds she might gaze upon that day and imagined what it would feel like to fly. She made up new melodies in her head and dreamed of things like a fresh rainfall and appreciated the morning sunrise.

Moral of the story: Be more like Helga.

The salt block should be almost completely heated up by now. A tiny splash of water should bounce off the stone if it's hot enough. Slice the radishes and remaining mushrooms into thin flat, fully rounded coins. Imagine them like thin coins that will brown ever so slightly and be used as a condiment on the burgers. Lay them on the salt block, leaving a small amount of space on the left-hand side of the block for the flip and roll. Try to fit as many as you can on your block but know it might take two sessions of cooking to get the mushrooms and radishes all cooked. Once they are laid on the block, drizzle a swoop of oil up and down the block for added moisture and listen to it sizzle. The salt will settle into each of the ingredients and make for the absolutely perfect amount of flavor.

Drizzle a large open skillet lightly with olive oil and prepare to cook the burgers over a medium heat, grill, or open fire. Lay the burgers flat on your pan.

Check back in with the mushrooms and radishes and give them a turn and a nudge on the block. Once the mushrooms and radishes are slightly browned on both sides, remove them from the heat, and set aside.

Check back in with the burgers, flipping and even peeking into the center of the burger to check the color.

Layer as follows: woodland-like whole wheat bun, Spicy Homemade Mustard or flavorful condiment of choice, a thin layer of foraged fungi and slightly browned rainbow radishes, live micro greens or moss-like sprouts, burger, fresh slice of heirloom tomato, and poppy seeds. Devour.

Imagine how one could serve up this meal! On a sliced tree stump with bubbly beers on the side. With a fresh side salad of arugula and simplified nuts and berries! Chilled honey lemonade or maple syrup baked beans with fresh juicy seedless watermelon! I can taste the forest and the sunshine! Oh, the wilderness tastes so good.

SPICY HOMEMADE MUSTARD

Combine the water, maple syrup, honey, vinegar, mustard seed, and cayenne (see page 231 for more condiments and sauces).

SPICY HOMEMADE MUSTARD

$^{1}/_{4}$ cup water

2 tablespoons maple syrup

2 tablespoons raw honey

1 tablespoon apple cider vinegar

$^{1}/_{4}$ cup yellow mustard seeds

$^{1}/_{4}$ teaspoon cayenne

Wild Clover Rice

1¾ cups water

1 cup forbidden rice

Pinch of salt

½ pound carrots

¼ pound celery

1 cup foraged wild clover flowers

Honey or maple syrup

1 tablespoon butter or to taste

NOTE: Red clover is generally not recommended to be consumed by pregnant women, so it might be something to look forward to postpartum.

One summer, we spent a month up north at a cabin on the lake with the girls. We fished and dug our toes in the sand, doused our bodies in the water, and spent more time doing "nothing," which in turn felt like everything. We took a drive into the small town to get groceries and on our way back, we stopped on the side of the road to gather up a basket full of wild red clover. We gently plucked the tops of the flowers off, sharing scissors back and forth, and chatted with my oldest daughter, Luella, about each petal and stem. "There's another one!" It was pure roadside delight and experiencing her excitement with each clipping was equally as satisfying. There were thousands of them, covering each side of the road and ranging from deep purple to a lighter pink toward the base of the flower. Their floral heads ranged in size from smaller than an inch to a bit more than an inch across and spread out in different directions. Clovers bloom in late spring and continue their blossom all throughout the summer and sometimes even into October. Their habitat can be roadsides, grassy or weedy areas in the city or countryside, meadows, backyard lawns, or pastures. Be sure to pay attention if there are chemicals sprayed, especially if you find them close to suburban or city locales. Clover is one of nature's blooming delights, bursting everywhere.

Combine the water with the rice and a pinch of salt. Bring to a boil over high heat. Cover, reduce heat, and simmer for 30 minutes.

Chop the carrots and celery into small dices. For a seasonal lunch, keep the carrots and celery raw and crisp and for a seasonal dinner, caramelize the carrots and celery with a small amount of oil or butter in a pan over medium heat. Chop half of the clover flowers.

Remove the rice from heat and mix in the chopped and full clover flowers. Let stand covered for a few minutes. Add in the chopped vegetables. Drizzle the honey. Braid in the amount of butter to your liking. Fluff and devour. Simple. Magical.

Chilled Rainbow Quinoa

3 cups water

1½ cups rainbow quinoa

5 leaves fresh kale

16 ounces smoked salmon fillet (enough to make about 2 cups chopped)

1 red pepper

Enoki mushrooms (enough to make about 1½ cups chopped)

2 cloves Preserved Garlic (see page 241)

3 tablespoons apple cider vinegar

3 tablespoons olive oil

1 tablespoon maple syrup

¼ teaspoon sea salt

1 cup dried cranberries

1 cup feta cheese

Consider doubling this recipe to have giant lunch bowls on hand throughout the week! It's a simple one that can be stored in the fridge and used for a quick meal before exploring the outdoors. It's a perfect nature-based dish to serve at a baby or bridal shower and one to introduce to the little ones once they are able to chew solid foods.

Bring water to a boil, then pour in the quinoa, and turn down the heat to medium to simmer. Cover the pan and wait about 20 minutes or until all the water is absorbed. Turn the heat off and keep the pan covered to finish steaming.

While the quinoa is cooking, pull the kale apart, discarding the stems, and then tear and break the leaves into small pieces, noticing the curled edges and deep lustrous color of green. Chop the smoked salmon, red pepper, and enoki mushrooms into perfect bite-size portions. Crush and chop the preserved garlic into fine pieces.

Add the apple cider vinegar, olive oil, maple syrup, and sea salt to a bowl. Pour the cooked quinoa into the bowl and mix in the kale, salmon, pepper, mushrooms, cranberries, and feta cheese. Fold them together so that all the ingredients are covered with the oils and juices evenly. Consider adding an extra splash of the type of consistency you are craving—throw in a dash extra of maple syrup if your mouth waters for more sweetness or splash in an extra burst of apple cider vinegar and salt if you want a cleanse for your gut.

Keep the leftovers refrigerated for 3 to 5 days. Freshen up by adding in a mix of fresh veggies or more kale.

Detox Dandelion Soup

"All you need is a little patience, a little work, and an open mind." I am wildly obsessed with Clara, the 98-year-old You-Tube sensation. She was the author of *Clara's Kitchen* and the host of an online cooking show called *Great Depression Cooking,* in which she talked about what she foraged and used while experiencing and living through the Great Depression. You can't help but love her. She had so little but maintained her gratitude, creativity, and curiosity for each ingredient. She carried a small knife with her at all times waiting for the opportune moment to harvest a dandelion, edible mushroom, or burdock or to pull something from her mother's garden. She believed that foraging and eating the way she did was part of why she lived for so long. In a day and age where we have offerings galore—grocery stores and restaurants seemingly at every corner of our towns, and services where almost any type of food is delivered to our door—there's a chance that we've lost the ability to view food as a simplistic form of nourishment. The harvest, the slow journey, and the depth of gratitude that is so essential to what fuels our bodies should all matter. She represents major goals for me, and I hope I am as chipper, agile, and curious at 98 years old as she was. I especially loved her foraging dandelion episode and the way the leaves looked so fresh and nourishing. She munched them with a dash of salt on top and seemed so happy.

This soft-as-silk soup is for all the rainy days and all the afternoons you just want to curl up on the couch and daydream and soak in warmth and a cleansing goodness. It's perfect for when you want to get lost in a thought instead of cutting perfectly squared pieces of vegetables. There's no need for perfection here—this is just a big bowl of cleanse and comfort.

Purslane, optimistic to the core, can be found to be thriving in poor soil. It's known to pop up in backyards, in cracks of heated sidewalks, in corners of a garden bed, or along the roadside. The tender, fat stems can be picked and washed and used in many dishes. The leaves and stems are rich in iron, vitamin A, vitamin C, calcium, and phosphorus. Rich in

recipe continues

3 garlic cloves

1 large onion (any allium will work!)

6 stalks celery

1 head of broccoli

Heaping handful of red radishes

1 large stalk fennel or foraged purslane (if available)

2 or 3 sprigs rosemary

Large bouquet of dandelion leaves

1 cup coconut oil

2 cups coconut milk

Salt and black pepper

3 tablespoons goat cheese

TOPPINGS

Goat cheese

Honey

Walnuts

Dandelion flowers or purslane

omega-3 fatty acids and antibacterial qualities, it makes for a perfect cleansing ingredient in this silky and delectable bowl of choice. Purslane is also available in season in many co-ops and farmers' markets.

The hairy-stemmed spurge is purslane's poisonous evil twin sister, so be sure to recognize and research your harvest fully! A mature spotted spurge variety will have a red tear-shaped spot in the middle of each leaf and a milky white production of sap when the stems are broken. Purslane is a succulent, white spurge is not. Always be 100 percent sure of what you forage.

———————————

Chop the garlic into fine pieces. Chop the onion, celery, broccoli, radish, and the wispy fronds and white bulb of the fennel or the stems of purslane. Use your fingers to peel down the leaves of the rosemary to separate them from the stem; chop the leaves finely. Chop the dandelion leaves into small pieces.

In a large pan, combine the coconut oil, garlic, onion, celery, and fennel or purslane. Sauté until the onions are slightly browned on all sides. Add the radish and dandelion leaves but leave out the broccoli for now! Bring it all to a boil over medium heat and simmer to soften them all. Add in the coconut milk. After about 15 to 25 minutes, toss in the broccoli and turn the heat off. Let sit for 5 to 10 minutes to soften the broccoli and cool.

In batches, pour or spoon the soup carefully into a blender. Add a pinch of salt, a bigger pinch of pepper, and the goat cheese. Then combine on medium speed.

Top with pinched-off sections of goat cheese, a drizzle of honey, a sprinkle of crushed walnuts, and some dandelion flowers or purslane for the creamiest cleansing soup.

Dandelions

Dandelions are best foraged in early spring or late autumn. They are like a cleansing ingredient for our bodies after the more sedentary, cozy lifestyle in the winter months or as preparation for the summer months ahead. The brightly colored dandelion is a sign of hope for new growth and a new season.

Every bit of the dandelion can be consumed. It's best to collect young leaves fresh from the ground but when possible, collect older dandelion roots, which, similar to wine and women, just get better with age. The leaves should not be bitter if foraged at the optimal peak of season. A bite into them will be enough to determine your timing but even if purchased from a co-op, the bitterness may still be present but that doesn't negate their benefits. When foraging (preferably after a fresh rain when the ground is moist and soft), put your hand gently around the small plant, taking your thumb and pointer finger at the base of the plant. Wiggle slowly and tug up toward the sky. Even a small root left in the ground will allow an additional dandelion to grow, leaving bounty for others. Honeybees have overflowing gratitude for the dandelion as they are sometimes the very first flowering plant it feeds on for pollen and nectar come spring. Let's be like the honeybee and express gratitude for this flowering plant!

To harvest dandelions with kindness, take your small knife and slice just at the base of the weed, leaving the root to regrow. Carry home and separate any dead portions or leaves from the fresh leaves. Snip the flowered heads and set aside. Rinse the leaves in cold water for a few minutes, tossing and turning and massaging the cold water into the crevices and folds of the leaf. Lay out flat on towel and set aside.

A cup of raw dandelion greens contains 112 percent of our daily required intake of vitamin A and 535 percent of vitamin K. The root, the stem, the flower, and the leaf can be prepared in a number of ways to work in connection with our body's needs and to supply nourishment. How marvelous and fascinating! This small weed, shunned and rejected in most lawns, can even be chopped, frozen, and stored away to blend into smoothies throughout any season. Dandelions are commonly sold at many co-ops these days as well, so if you aren't up for a romp in the dirt, gather them at your nearest co-op grocery store!

Sweet Potato Feast

1 cup red kidney beans
(raw or canned)

2 tablespoons maple
syrup

Smoked salt

1 large sweet potato

1 ear sweet corn

½ purple onion

Small bouquet of
flowering chives

Small bouquet
of fresh oregano

3 ounces dairy-free
cashew-milk herb cheese

2 tablespoons Earth
Balance vegan butter

Smoked pepper

NOTE: If this is
just for one person,
then you can make
it in a cast-iron
pan; otherwise lay
the ingredients out
on a sheet pan in
multiples for family
or guests!

A vegan summer mini feast for the inner bunny in you! I used to be not drawn to onions, yet the more I consumed them, the more my body craved them. I have always thought that our bodies, just like when training during exercise, will begin to want what we feed them. They can just as easily become addicted to raw onions as they would to sugar but we have to train them in a sense—although sugar is a wild one to retract, once it's been fed. This meal feels refreshing and simple and is an easy way to spruce up a "run of the mill" baked sweet potato. Gorgeous purple flowering chives, raw onions, homegrown oregano, and a baked sweet potato drizzled in olive oil and vegan butter served with a side of maple-soaked sprouted kidney beans. Bountiful. Simple. Magical. Nourishing.

Soak the kidney beans overnight, if raw. If they are canned, pull them out and drain them completely. Add them to a bowl, drizzle the maple syrup on top, and mix. Add a dash of salt, mix again, and let soak in. Set aside.

Preheat the oven to 400°F. With exuberance, stab the potato with a fork six or seven times, creating those small airways to the meat of the potato. Bake for 30 minutes.

Using a knife, slice the kernels off the corn, cutting away from you and down toward the cutting board. Turn and slice, turn and slice, until all the corn is gathered in a pile. Chop the onion, chives, and oregano into small pieces. Break apart the vegan cheese into separate sections. Set aside.

After 30 minutes, pull out the potatoes and gently slice a lowercase "l" down the middle of the potato and squeeze in the beans, corn, onions (reserving some for a topping), chives, oregano, and herb cheese. Burst it all into that potato! Let it overflow and tip out on the pan. Bake for an additional 10 to 13 minutes. Pull out and drizzle with butter, salt, pepper, and raw chopped onions.

If you consume dairy, feel free to opt for real grass-fed butter and creamy raw smoked cheddar cheese, and top with chopped bacon and extra black pepper!

Once upon a Queen Anne's Lace

There was a small lady. No, not a short human, she was a really small, red ladybug. Let's call her Miss Lady. She woke every morning to a roof of cloudy, frosted alabaster underbelly of blooms. It covered her like an umbrella. Her own personal dreamland. She lived under the center of a Queen Anne's lace flower.

She was the following (in no particular order):

Quiet

Kind

Generous

A little bit cautious

A little bit anxious

Peculiar

Slow

Curious

Smaller than the average ladybug

But, you say, how can that be? Ladybugs are already wildly small. Yes, I know, but she was even smaller than the smallest of the ladybugs. Her eyes popped out of her hard shell like bubbles, magnifying the world around her. She drifted through the world slowly and was never in a rush. When she flew, her wings expanded just barely half an inch into the air, but nevertheless they carried her from one world to the next, one bloom to the next. She didn't need much, just her miniature wings, a few friends, and the occasional sip of some honey. One morning, she decided to sew herself some itty-bitty slippers for her six legs. After all, her feet sometimes got cold. Out she went, flying around looking for some sort of material to make her slippers.

She flew until she spotted a red robin ahead. "Excuse me?" she squeaked to the robin. "Do you happen to have any extra string or wool left from your nest building? I was really hoping I could use a little to make myself some slippers." "Tweet!" said the robin, for she didn't speak ladybug.

Hmm, Miss Lady thought. And the robin flew away.

Her wings carried her down by the river, where she was certain she would be able to find something of substance to make her slippers. She met a turtle down there, basking in the sunshine. His shell looked dry and hot. "Hello there!" she said to the turtle. "I really hate to bother you, but I was wondering if you happened to have any dried out worms? I'm looking for some sort of material to make some slippers." The turtle just stared at Miss Lady. Miss Lady blinked back pleasantly. "Uh, hello?" she squeaked. He stared. *Oh,* she thought, *I guess perhaps he doesn't speak ladybug!* "I shall carry on!" she replied. She wasn't going to give up so soon.

She met a field cricket, a flower fly, and a forage looper moth. But no, they didn't speak ladybug either. She met an American bumblebee who gave her a sip of honey but he did not speak ladybug either! The day was hot and her teeny little wings were getting tired. She landed to rest right next to a group of banded woollybear caterpillar moths. *Gosh,* she thought, *one, two, three, four, five, six, seven, eight, nine, ten, eleven, twelve, thirteen, fourteen, fifteen, sixteen. They have sixteen legs each! There's no way they could make enough slippers for their feet and by the way, I bet they never get chilly feet anyway, because look at all that fur on their bodies.* She decided to not even bother them.

She flew up to the tallest maple tree to find the brightest pink rosy maple moth. "She must speak ladybug. She's just GOT to!" she whispered to herself. But the rosy maple moth was far too busy making her silky cocoon but, boy, was it pretty. Miss Lady sighed. Her wings had carried her so many miles that day and she thought, *Well, maybe I don't need new slippers after all.* She flew home, tucked herself back into the Queen Anne's

lace flower and just before falling asleep under the light of the moon, her eyes boggled open big. Even bigger than they already were. She looked around and whispered, "Hey, what if I already have everything I need?" She burst from her slumber and started pulling down small bits of Queen Anne's lace and weaving the layers of creamed petals with strands and stems. After much concentration, she had braided her very own warm slippers. What she had longed for to make her happy was simply right in front of her.

QUEEN ANNE'S LACE IDENTIFYING POINTS

- Hairy stem

- A single purple or black dot-like center

- A flat umbrel (the umbrella-like flowering top)

- Fernlike leaves with hairy bottoms

- Long, pronglike bases below the flowers

- Condensed group of white blooms

Lace Jelly

3 cups tightly pressed Queen Anne's lace flowers

6 cups water

4½ cups organic cane sugar

1 cup fresh lemon juice

2 packets pectin (optional)

I've given it a lot of thought and have officially decided that Queen Anne's lace is my favorite bloom! If I had to be surrounded by one flower for the rest of my life, it would be those creamy and bursting-with-life blossoms. I love the way they dance in the wind ever so gently and subtly. I love their fresh and soft aroma of carrot. I love their tone of green, their fern-shaped leaf, and the way their heart-opening white top broadens toward the sky.

Queen Anne's lace is a hairy-stemmed biennial. It grows on roadsides and in fields, backyards, and parks. It often has a purple dot in its center and flowers May through October. Be sure to take the time to identify Queen Anne's lace blooms as they wildly resemble poison hemlock, which is absolutely not safe to consume. The roots and leaves are also edible, but this recipe is focused on the flowers.

Lace Jelly has become a summer favorite of mine over the years and one that I look forward to processing with the girls through the warm months.

Once you have foraged the flowers safely, take them home and snip the flower heads. Bring the water to a boil, then turn off heat. Steep the flowers, like a tea, in the hot water for at least 30 minutes. Strain. Add in the sugar, lemon juice, and pectin (if using), bring to a boil, and stir constantly for a few minutes. Transfer into another pot for small batch boils. The surface area of the smaller pot will allow it to thicken much better and not lose as much moisture. Bring it to a roaring boil for around 1 minute each.

Sterilize glass jars and lids by bathing them in a medium to hot pan of water. Pour contents into the jars with ¼-inch headspace. Place on the lids, soak, and process in hot water for 5 minutes to seal. Let sit for 24 hours before mixing around to allow it to set.

The flavor is earth meets a hint of sweet and one of my absolute seasonal favorites! Enjoy, store, or give away.

A Salad Fit for a Queen

2 fresh handfuls
of fresh lettuce

1 fresh white fennel bulb

¼ head white cauliflower

½ cup chopped white
radishes

½ cup chopped medjool
dates

½ cup white chocolate-
covered raisins or almonds

Medium-size bouquet
of Queen Anne's lace

Driving through the country one summer along the river, I discovered blooming on the roadside the largest field of tall, white lace that went from the edge of the gravel line all the way down a hill. It stretched out and extended so far, I had to pull over and see it closer. The small, pale white buds swayed back and forth in the wind like lightning bugs in the daytime. They had a single dark-colored floret just off the center of their bloom that was just a pencil size dot. I sat among the flowers there in the dirt, wearing my favorite green high-waisted skirt, and they towered 4 feet above me. I was able to see the underlying lines that connected the stem to the bloom—those lines may be my favorite part about the plant, so straight and rigid and somehow firm. I had everywhere to be, but I just set that all aside and sat with the roadside blooms for a little bit longer. What is life, if we cannot slow down for a moment here or there?

Queen Anne's lace is known as "wild carrot" or "bird's nest" and is a native wildflower herb that grows in many parts of the world and can grow up to 4 feet tall. This salad is white and bright and most delightful. It somehow has a feminine feel. Even if Queen Anne's lace is not currently in season, you can replace the blooms with a handful of edible white rose petals, daisy petals, or fennel blooms to enjoy all season long.

Lay out the lettuce in a serving bowl. Chop the end of the root of the fennel bulb and continue to make thin cuts and slices. Layer on top of the greens, like freshly cut ribbons! Slice off the stem of the cauliflower, pull apart the florets, and chop into small edible pieces. Mince the radishes and dates into small sections and sprinkle them in a circular motion over the greens and fennel. Take a handful of white chocolate-covered raisins or almonds and sprinkle on as if this was a dessert! Tuck in the full blooms of Queen Anne's lace and indulge in the salad on its own or pair it with a blush or poppy seed dressing!

The Freshest Fiddlehead Fern Flatbread

Lush, green ferns bloom with great bounty on the land of the Bear's parents. They live on a lake with birch trees tucking their log home in just right, and the ferns become alive throughout the summer. Their ferns bloom bigger than I could grasp with my arms out wide. His mom is kinder than humans come and his dad is more charming and wise than one could imagine. The Bear's grandma cared for many plants and animals, but the ferns stood out as one of her favorite earth-grown goods. To this day, we talk of her powerfully calm spirit, and every spring and summer the bountiful ferns remind us of her. She had the same form of unforced strength and utter acceptance for all that the Bear's parents have. I want to be like that.

Fiddleheads are the first to arrive on the crown of the fern. The most common fern is the ostrich fern. They are best harvested at 2 to 6 inches high, when they are both tasty and curled. Harvesting some from each plant maintains the growth for the current year and for next year's foraging. It's important to use a straight knife and get a solid cut across, so as to not damage the fern's potential for growth. The flavor is similar to that of asparagus or green beans, depending on the harvest and individual fern. To avoid potential digestive tenderness, they should always be cleaned and cooked appropriately to avoid bitterness and to maintain their taste and color. You'll find these sold in the spring at about the same time that morel mushrooms can be foraged. Morels grow in the county, the city, the forest, and the suburbs. They pop up on many occasions and are almost married to the fiddlehead fern in terms of seasonal availability.

This flatbread is a refreshing burst of welcome to spring. It has hints of sweetness and is uplifting, yet carries an underlying spicy earthy flavor—the best of both worlds on top of soft, fluffy, breaded goodness.

recipe continues

2 cups fiddlehead ferns

1 cup cherry tomatoes

¼ cup pitted castelvetrano olives

1 firm blood orange

1 firm grapefruit

1 large flatbread

Light and Bright Sauce (see below)

1 cup feta cheese

1½ cups mint leaves

1 lemon or 1 tablespoon lemon juice

¼ cup olive oil

¼ pound spiced ground bison or spiced sausage (optional)

Preheat the oven to 425°F. Wash the fiddlehead ferns; bring a pot of water to a boil and immerse the fiddleheads for 5 to 8 minutes until the tannins and bacterias are boiled away. Rinse in cold water and set aside to cool. On medium heat, cook the spiced sausage and set aside to cool.

Chop the cherry tomatoes in quarters and the olives in halves. Peel both the blood orange and the grapefruit by hand. Then, using a serrated knife, slice the blood orange and grapefruit into thin edible bites with gentle, quick cuts so as not to mash up their citrus elements too much.

Lay out the flatbread and spoon on the Light and Bright Sauce, curving and rounding each corner of the flatbread. Massaging it into the dough and breathing in the most refreshing scent of mint is the celebratory essence of this life. We are alive! Isn't that amazing!? Spread the spiced sausage out evenly. Grab the fiddlehead ferns and lay out in a pattern of your choosing on the flatbreads. Lines, circles, no rhyme or reason—just go with what's inside of you. Next, top with the tomatoes, olives, blood orange, grapefruit, and feta. A sprinkle here, an even sprinkle there. Peel fresh mint leaves off their stem and sprinkle on top. Cut a lemon in half. Zing, my mouth is watering! Squeeze the juice all over, erupting with intention and gratitude. Pour the olive oil evenly over.

Bake in the oven for 8 to 12 minutes, until just slightly browned and the feta cheese is perfectly melted.

Offer the Light and Bright Yogurt sauce on the side for those extra leftover crust pieces that everyone always leaves on their plate. Consume it all and leave no crumbs behind!

LIGHT AND BRIGHT SAUCE

1 cup plain, whole milk Greek yogurt

2 tablespoons olive oil

½ cup mint leaves

¼ teaspoon cumin

Pinch of salt

1 capful of apple cider vinegar

In a food processor, combine the yogurt, olive oil, mint, cumin, salt, and apple cider vinegar. Blend until combined, then set aside in the refrigerator until ready to use!

Bone Broth

2 pounds of bones (you can use the bones from chicken, beef, duck, turkey, wild caught fish, goose, or deer)

Slightly chilled water

3 tablespoons apple cider vinegar

1 onion

1 stalk celery

½ pound carrots

3 to 5 garlic cloves

Bouquet of parsley

Herb of choice

Pinch of salt and black pepper

Bone broth is an absolute essential for cold winters. Stocking the freezer with bone broth is something that has become a regular occurrence for us after hearing about this process a few winters back from my friend who lived on a farm near us. The simplicity of this recipe, the amount of time it takes, and the absolute nourishment that it provides is beyond incredible. When sickness strikes, it's available to indulge in or serve to my family and pairs well with a soft cotton blanket on the couch or in a to-go mug for a brisk and effervescent walk in the woods.

Since you will be extracting nourishment from the bones of these animals, the most important aspect will be the health of the animals. Choosing organic, grass-fed, and home-grown animals will increase the strength and nourishment of the bone broth. In addition, there will be less foam produced and fewer impurities that float to the top.

Set the bones into an 8-quart pot and pour the chilled water to completely cover them. Add the apple cider vinegar and let sit for 5 to 10 minutes to encourage the nutrition of the bones to come out. Turn the stove onto medium heat and bring to a simmer. Chop up the onions, celery, and carrots, crush the garlic cloves, and add them all to the pot. Bring to a boil for a few minutes and then back down to a low simmer. Add more water if needed and cook for about 2 hours. Remove the impurities and foam that rise to the top of the pot and discard. The healthier the animal, the fewer impurities there will be to remove. Remove the vegetables and bones if desired. Consume immediately or put into sterilized glass jars to freeze and don't forget to leave a little room on top for expansion.

Magic Fairy Blush Soup

Himalayan salt block

5 small sweet potatoes

5 small white potatoes

3 small to medium beets

1 purple onion

1 apple

1 piece fresh ginger root

2 garlic cloves

10 to 15 stems fresh thyme

2 tablespoons butter

Himalayan salt stone, about the size of a big acorn

4 cups water or bone broth

Salt

2 handfuls of in-season foraged mushrooms

Olive oil

3 tablespoons arrowroot powder or crushed and dried cattail roots

4 tablespoons beet powder

2 cups English peas

Fresh torn parsley, raw cheddar, or honey goat cheese, for serving

A most magical stew with the most beautiful blush color that is perfect to serve to others. Being able to describe the ingredients that are scooped up on the spoon is a fairylike scavenger hunt. The stew is sweet and savory and warm and somehow feels fancy. Served with warm bread spread with butter with sprinkled beet powder on top, it makes for a feast fit for a fairy family!

I prefer to keep the skin on my potatoes and apples to keep all the nutrition that the plant can offer, but peel the skin away if you prefer. If we find the produce in the woods, fresh off a tree or bursting from the ground, we consume nearly the entire plant. We view the entire whole as nourishment and wouldn't think about peeling the skin away.

With so many ingredients sprawled on the table, it makes for a most delightful meal to engage fully with. The Himalayan salt block liberates its qualities deep up into the pores of the mushrooms and browns them just ever so slightly as to offer a variation in texture in this soup.

Stack two stove grates on top of one another, place the Himalayan salt block on top of the two grates. Turn on a low heat to begin to warm the stone.

Put out a large bowl to gather all the vegetables (not including the mushrooms) as they are chopped, chopped, chopped! Slice the sweet potatoes and white potatoes into spoonsize edible bits. During spring and summer, peel the potatoes and make the cuts small and petite. Through fall and winter, wash the skins, keep the peels attached, and make the cuts chunkier and thicker. This turns the dish into one that requires grabbing a big spoon from the drawer and somehow feels warmer and cozier, if that is even imaginable! I am secretly obsessed with using the big spoons. Chop the beets, onions, apple, ginger, and garlic into small cubes. Peel the leaves of the thyme off the stem and chop finely. The heavy amount of thyme is one of my favorite elements about this dish. Add all to the bowl. On

recipe continues

the stovetop, heat the butter until melted and pour over the vegetables to caramelize just slightly.

Pour the water or bone broth into a 5- to 8-quart pot along with the vegetables and a dash of salt. Add the small Himalayan salt stone on low heat.

Brush any dirt off the mushrooms and slice the stems off. Do not soak them as they quickly become waterlogged and tend to lose some of their flavor. Slice into flat, coin-like shapes. Test out the salt block by splashing a dash of water on top. If it's ready to use, the water should sizzle just slightly and bounce right off the block. Place the mushroom slices on the warmed Himalayan salt block, leaving room on the left side for the flip and turn. Drizzle with a dash of olive oil and listen to the sizzle! Once browned on both sides, chop into quarters and combine with the stew over low heat.

Arrowroot powder is an amazingly easy-to-digest thickening ingredient that derives from the arrowroot plant—a very hardy, clump-forming perennial plant with thick stalks up to 6 feet high and large bright green leaves 12 to 24 inches long. The roots are harvested, then dried and ground into a powderlike form. To use, separately heat equal parts water and powder, stir to make a paste, and then pour into the soup.

Keep the English peas aside to be thrown in close to the end of the cooking. They add a burst of variation, texture, and delight!

Stir the soup often and allow the salt stone to exude its magic. Serve with fresh torn parsley, more chopped thyme, raw cheddar, or honey goat cheese on top! A blush-toned, warm delight.

FOR A CHILLED SUMMER VERSION, cook extra long the night before so the vegetables are all exceptionally soft. Blend in the blender the following day and serve as a purée with thinly sliced beets and a dollop of sour cream or plain Greek yogurt on top! Refreshing!

FOR A SIMPLIFIED VERSION, combine 2 cups water or bone broth, 3 or 4 chopped sweet potatoes, 1 chopped beet, 1 cup chopped mushrooms, 1 garlic clove, 1 cup peas, 3 stems fresh thyme, 2 tablespoons beet powder, and ½ tablespoon ginger powder and heat until the vegetables are tender.

Garlic Scape Wreath Pasta

2 pounds garlic scapes, about 12-18 of similar size

1 head purple cabbage

5 to 7 carrots

1 large fennel stalk

Small bouquet of fresh parsley

1 cup sunflower oil

1 teaspoon garlic salt

4 quarts water

Pinch of salt

12 ounces spinach or butternut squash linguini

1 cup feta

½ lemon

The way my mom wove intrigued me. I stared up at the tall wooden table in awe as she tucked and pulled and tied and braided, weaving each strand of dirty brown twig in and out of one another, then swiftly moving to pick up another branch and placing it in tenderly but with a sort of strength and vision. That's just the kind of person that she is. How she is able to exude both tenderness and strength simultaneously, I will never know, but I want to be like that. My mom was my first visual teacher in wreath making, although I don't remember her sitting and walking me through each step. It was as if it was soaked, downloaded, or catalogued into my brain by virtue of being her budding offspring.

When woven into a wreath or bird's nest, garlic scapes tangibly breathe inspiration in the kitchen like the magic of a floral workshop. Garlic scapes, flower buds of the garlic plant, are curly and twisted and wild and free. They offer incredible amounts of protein, vitamin C, calcium, and antioxidants, and their taste is entrancing! They are long, thin, grass-colored, and ribbonlike delights that can be used similarly to garlic—eaten raw or cooked in a dish.

Feel free to omit the pasta and simply soak in the goodness of earth-grown goods.

To begin, straighten out six scapes, holding the bases with one hand and pulling the ends out. Have someone hold the ends and very loosely braid them. Loose! Loose! Free flowing! Tie the ends together with baker's twine, as if you were making a floral head crown. This is easiest to do with a second pair of hands and makes an amazing "couples date night" project. Inviting your children into this beauteous process is also rewarding. Repeat this process, braiding the next grouping of scapes a little less tight so there is variation. Again, like a floral head crown! Lay the two wreaths on a sheet pan on top of one another, tucking the smaller one inside the larger one.

recipe continues

Chop the cabbage in thin rows so that the pieces easily fall apart like ribbons, loosely and freely. Separate them and set aside. Using a peeler or peeling machine, peel the carrots with long ribbonlike light strokes to create thin strips. Pull apart all of the flowing branched sections of the fennel. Chop the base of the bulb, and then starting from the bottom of the bulb, chop in thin sections so the alabaster white pieces of the bulb fall and disconnect. Chop the parsley and set aside.

Preheat the oven to 425°F.

Once there are piles of separated, ribbonlike cabbage, carrots, and fennel surrounding you, tap into your floral design skills. I believe everyone has them deep inside somewhere! Take a piece of one of the vegetable strips and begin tucking and pulling and layering and weaving them into the wreaths—let loose, pull tight. Braid and imagine. Once all of the vegetable strips have been incorporated into the wreaths, drizzle with $1/2$ cup of the sunflower oil and sprinkle with the garlic salt. Bake for 20 to 23 minutes, or until the garlic scapes show signs of browning edges.

About halfway through baking, fill a pot with 4 quarts of water and the salt and bring to a boil. Cook the linguini for 4 minutes. Drain, put on a large platter, and drizzle the other $1/2$ cup sunflower oil on top. Pull the scape wreath from the oven and set on top of the linguini. Sprinkle with the fresh parsley, feta, and squeezed lemon juice. Oh! My mouth is watering.

Serve with a crisp, dry Pinot Grigio white wine.

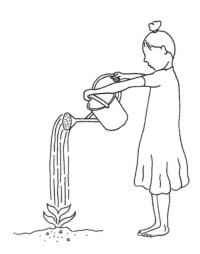

Sweet Pea Salad

2 eggs

1½ cups arugula

1½ cups spinach

1 cup chopped button
mushrooms

1 blood orange

1 tablespoon bee pollen

¼ cup raw walnuts

¼ cup raw pumpkin seeds

½ cup English peas

2 sprigs of rosemary

Sunflower Blush Dressing
(see page 237)

I've always felt like salads are the only food you can completely stuff your face with and still look classy. For example, when I see someone smashing their face with greens, the only thing I ever think is, "Yeah! You get it!" I absolutely love oversize green salads for lunch for the way they carry me through that afternoon bump.

This salad is incredibly bountiful and green! Most all these items can be grown at home or found in any grocery store large or small. The English peas can be exchanged for any peas, but there's something about the pop and crunch that they offer—similar to the pop of a sugar snap—that works really well! Fresh rosemary is a bite of earth.

Bring 2 cups of water to boil and gently place in 2 eggs to hard-boil. Boil for 7 minutes then turn the heat off and allow to sit in the water for 2 minutes. Then rinse under cold water and set aside.

Lay out the arugula and spinach greens flat on a plate. Chop or rip apart the mushrooms and lay on top of the bed of greens. Peel or slice the blood orange and set on the side of the plate. Sprinkle on the bee pollen, walnuts, pumpkin seeds, and fresh crisp peas. Lay the rosemary sprigs out on the side, pull each of the leaves from the stem, and sprinkle onto the greens. Once the eggs have cooled, peel, chop into edible bites, and sprinkle on the salad. Prepare a side of brown rice or quinoa to pair alongside.

An earth cleanse. Yes!

Spicy Grouse Tacos

2 purple bell peppers

Bouquet of red radishes

3 stalks lemongrass

Olive oil

Garlic powder

Black pepper

Salt

Bouquet of cilantro

8 ounces aged white
cheddar

1 jalapeño pepper

2 to 4 grouse breasts

1 tablespoon cumin

¼ teaspoon chili powder

2 fresh garlic cloves

5 to 10 sprouted whole
grain tortillas

2 limes

1 cup organic sour cream

In Minnesota, there are more than 10,000 lakes. According to the Minnesota Department of Natural Resources, there are 11 million acres of public hunting land, 528 designated hunting areas in the ruffed grouse range, covering nearly 1 million acres, more than 40 designated ruffed grouse management areas, and 600 miles of hunter walking trails.

Grouse hunting in the Midwest is an absolute art and a most formidable challenge. It's something to be embraced as a hunter, making the journey all the more rewarding and the harvest further expanded by gratitude. The hunter visits the woods each fall, but must seek out where the birds live. There are no creative ways that currently exist to attract the birds to the hunters—no place where hunters are "likely to find them." It's foraging at its finest and ultimately requires having an open-minded perspective. Grouse prefer young forests, which, like children, don't stay young forever. The hunt is an outstanding reminder of the incomparable art of being connected to this earth and keeping one's mind observant, wild, and open to the innate listening of the heart and direction of the woods.

Grouse offers lean nutrition with about 140 calories, 24 grams of protein, and 1 gram of fat, depending on the size of the bird. If there aren't grouse available in your region, pheasants, quail, or turkey are generally easily obtainable in local high-end supermarkets. Even chicken can be subbed, although the taste will be remarkably less wild.

Cut the purple peppers into thin long slices and place them into a small bowl. Coin the radishes into very thin paperlike slices and place into the bowl. In this same bowl, add circles of thinly sliced fresh lemongrass, drizzle on some olive oil, and sprinkle on garlic, black pepper, and salt.

Mince the cilantro and place in a separate mini bowl. Grate the aged white cheddar cheese and place into a separate bowl also! With care, slice the jalapeño pepper and place into a separate bowl. Include a few seeds if your guests are extra brave, and leave them out if they might be drawn to a milder but bold heat.

Slice the thawed breast of the grouse into thin, long sections. Consider gratitude for the life of this small animal. Put the meat and some olive oil in a seasoned cast-iron pan and add the cumin and chili powder. Crush and mince the garlic, add to the pan, and let it flavor the grouse as it cooks. Heat each side of the meat on high heat, flipping to brown, about 5 minutes each side.

Form the tortillas into bowl-like shapes and set inside unbleached coffee filters. To display premade tacos, set two or three of these inside each guest's bowl and fill with the prepared ingredients. Otherwise offer the ingredients for everyone to dig into—the meat, bright colored and spicy peppers, flexible radishes, lemongrass, cilantro, cheese, limes, and sour cream. There are many ways to do this!

Wildflower Honeycomb Artichokes

Himalayan salt block

2 artichokes

2 tablespoons olive oil

½ pound enoki mushrooms

¼ cup wildflower comb honey

1 tablespoon bee pollen

½ tablespoon salt

½ tablespoon black pepper

2 cups water

Notice the folds of an artichoke. It's like a flower with the most vibrant color, tone, and texture. The artichoke has always inspired me and becomes a delicate treat when paired with honey. I became obsessed with the way my kitchen sounds as the mushrooms simmer on top of a salt cooking block. Bee pollen is considered one of nature's most completely nourishing foods because it contains nearly all nutrients required by humans. Wildflower comb honey is a brightly flavored, intriguing, and gorgeous source of fatty acids. Notice its hexagonal wax structure. It looks like a fairytale. Document patterns in nature. Appreciate them!

Stack two stove grates on top of one another, place the Himalayan salt block on top, and turn on a low heat to warm. Heat on low for 15 minutes, then turn up to medium/high heat for another 10 minutes.

Wash the artichokes thoroughly and cut off the stems so they are able to stand with their tops toward the sky. Pull apart the mushroom cluster from their stem to individual mushrooms. Begin simmering on the heated salt block with 1 tablespoon of the olive oil. I think you'll enjoy this sizzling noise. Flip and let the salt simmer away into the depths of each mushroom.

Tuck and braid each mushroom into the folds of the artichoke. Experience this. Let them hang loose and wild as if you were designing a wreath made of blooms. Drizzle the honey into the folds of the artichoke. Sprinkle with bee pollen, salt, and pepper. The goal is to encourage the artichoke leaves to stay moist and soft.

Bring the water to a boil in a pot and steam the artichokes over medium heat for 15 minutes. Keep the pot covered to allow the steam to work its most moist magic. Serve and delight in the tastes, flavors, and curious offering on the plate by peeling off each leaf and spooning out the artichoke meat. Deeper into the center of the artichoke will produce more meat and flavor.

Chapter 4
DINNER

Chanterelle Bacon Brussels Sprouts

2 brussels sprout stalks, or 8 cups sprouts

24 ounces bacon

Small bouquet of sage

1½ cups chopped fresh foraged chanterelles (or 2 cups dried)

1 cup olive oil

One season it rained and rained and rained, and I couldn't stay out of the woods. It was getting to the point where everyone would be inside the house, and I would say to the Bear, "Oh, I have to check something really quick outside. I'll be right back!" Then I'd dodge down the same entrance to the woods that I am always drawn to. The grasses leaned to each side and opened up like a welcoming. The biggest tree leaned over on its side as if it might fall someday but its roots went deep down toward the earth. The small, golden bursts of edible chanterelles would shine through the brown soaking wet leaves, and I would scrape my hands through the piles to try to find as many as I could. The gills flowed up from the base of the stem toward the underbelly of the cap. I was leery because of their size and debated whether I should let them grow for a day or so more, or if they'd be eaten by deer while I slept. I drove myself mad in the debate. I wanted to dig mini posts and build a fence around them for my own. They smelled of faint apricot and had grown taller by two mornings later so we gathered them inside.

Preheat the oven to 400°F.

Lay the brussels sprout stalks onto a parchment-lined sheet pan. Take the uncooked bacon and wrap the slices around the vibrant green stalks—tucking and curving around each bubbled sprout, resting here and lying there, and utilizing toothpicks for stabilization. Brush on the olive oil. Chop the sage leaves and foraged mushrooms small enough to sprinkle. Sprinkle the mushrooms, sage, and pinch of salt on the stalks with your fingertips. Bake for 30 minutes.

Serve these full stalk; otherwise remove the toothpicks, lean the stalk in the upright position, and use a knife to chop off the individual sprouts onto a platter or into a bowl with the bacon and mushrooms.

Deep, Dark Venison Chili

7 to 10 carrots

½ stalk celery

1½ cups chopped
in-season foraged
mushrooms

½ cup butter, plus
1 tablespoon

1 pound ground venison
or ground beef

Small bouquet of oregano

½ cup crushed cashews

6 small purple potatoes

2 cans crushed tomatoes
or 5 to 7 heirloom
tomatoes, boiled down

2 cups canned black
beans, drained

2 cups canned kidney
beans, drained

3 cups water

3 tablespoons chili
powder

3 tablespoons cumin

1 tablespoon cayenne
pepper

Black pepper

Crushed red pepper

1½ cups brewed dark
roast coffee or espresso

As the air changes from warm and muggy to cool and crisp, I can't help but feel a little giddy. The meals on the table shift from light and bright to dark and deep. Root vegetables join spiced beans, and warm stews simmer on the stove as the cool breezes stream into the house. Let's be real—the country mice also start looking for warmer corners, and the girls wonder why we can't keep them and live out our own little Cinderella story with friends.

Begin by chopping up the carrots, celery, and half of the mushrooms into small edible bites. Through spring and summer, I chop the pieces finer, and all through fall and winter, I leave them chunkier and bolder. Place the ½ cup butter in the bottom of a large stockpot over medium heat until the butter begins to sizzle. Add the vegetables and mix. Watch them start to soften and caramelize, brown with the butter sinking into them, then turn to a low heat.

Place 1 tablespoon butter on a cast-iron pan, turn to high, and lay small strips of venison on top to sizzle on each side, leaving them slightly rare. Remove to a plate to add later.

Peel the leaves off the oregano, chop them ever so finely, and add to the sizzling pot of vegetables. Chop the cashews into small pieces and add to the pot. Cooked cashews offers such a variation and surprise and hints of nut flavor that pairs well with the deep dark elements of this chili. Chop the potatoes, and combine with the vegetables.

When most of the moisture has left the pot but just before the vegetables begin to stick to the bottom, add the tomatoes, beans, and water. Add the chili powder, cumin, and peppers. Let simmer. Stir every once in awhile and watch for a slow boil to erupt. Test the potatoes to check for your preferred consistency. About 10 minutes before completion, pour in the coffee or espresso and cooked venison. Stir once again.

Explore with this recipe and engage with flavors you are most drawn to. Opt for more cumin or less coffee. Play with a

1¹⁄₂ raw foraged in-season mushrooms

8 ounces grated raw smoked cheddar cheese

Raw onion, diced

Dash of smoked alder salt

heavy sprinkling of black pepper or a light sprinkling of crushed red pepper.

Serve by an outdoor fire in big mugs, with big spoons, and add fresh foraged mushrooms, raw smoked cheddar cheese, small diced raw onion, and a dash of smoked alder salt on top.

Seeding Togetherness

One afternoon we were packing up to move out of our little green home in a small town. Among the busy moments of stuffing objects into unlabeled and disheveled boxes, I noticed my neighbor out washing his car, as neighbors sometimes do. We had lived there for 3 years, which felt like an eternity for a free-spirited, wandering, "don't lock me down" type. But this man had lived there his whole life. He grew up in this home, now with his two grown children, and the house was passed down from his parents and their parents before them. He grew up playing and running in the same grass he now mowed. His loyalty to the space intrigued me.

I had never appreciated or even noticed the giant maple tree in his front yard. It struck me that day. I paused. My head tipped so far back and my eyes to the sky. There is no denying the pacifying appeal of the under-belly of a collection of maple leaves. Their shape alone, if we observe long enough, becomes entrancing and interesting. Anything can become interesting if we allow it to be. My neighbor and I didn't talk a ton throughout the years we lived there other than a courteous hello and goodbye and a nod during the cold months. We were in opposite spectrums of our life, his kids all grown and mine needing me every spare moment. We were friendly, but he wasn't the neighbor we sat with and pulled weeds beside. (That was 80-year-old Adelaide. But that's a story for another day.) In that small moment we connected over that tree. I continued to stare and finally let out my examinations. "This tree is so beautiful," I said. He immediately perked up. You could tell it had special meaning. Among the memories he had at that home and the dedication he had for the property, he took greatest delight in this tree when he spoke

of it. His eyes got slightly brighter and he even took a few steps toward me. He said, "Yes! This one!" I stepped closer as well. He went on, "This tree was only 2 feet tall when we planted it so many years ago. You see, my wife and children bought it for me for Father's Day one year. We came out here with their small shovels to dig. I'll never forget that day."

The tree was so large now. It reached much higher than the height of their cream-colored home. It was truly beautiful. Even more beautiful because its roots had been watered by the family of four. What an amazing wonder it must have been to have watched that tree grow. I imagined him and his wife having those small moments where you just look at your kids and realize, they're so grown. How did you grow so fast? Life sweeps by until the next pause when that sentence is repeated, but now those small lives are no longer babies or toddlers, they are close to adolescents. The small sapling tree grew right along with the family. Then one day that tree was so strong and stable that it didn't need the stakes any-more to hold it up or to be checked out quite as often as it did when it was young. Some maple trees are slow growers, taking 20 to 30 years to reach full size, and some are fast growers, taking 10 to 15 years. The duration of time doesn't matter as long as they are healthy and happy.

A diameter of 12 inches is the minimum requirement the trunk must reach before tapping for maple syrup. So if we all plant a maple tree this year, then either our own family or future ones will be able to harvest its goodness for maple syrup when it's ready in the spring. These are all small steps toward a greater connection with the earth. Early autumn is a great time to plant a maple tree. As the cooler temperatures are welcomed in, the leaves will fall and the focus for root growth remains. The Arbor Day Foundation notes that members of this species can grow as far south as United States Department of Agriculture Plant Hardiness Zone 8, though they may not produce sugar due to the lack of freezing temperatures. Maple flavors can vary among caramel, vanilla, nutty, buttery, floral, and chocolate, and even hints of a coffee flavor can be found in some syrups. Maple syrup is similar to wine in the sense that there are variables in flavor based on soil and the production of syrup. These variations should be sampled, noted, and appreciated. Some maples have been known produce sap for several generations, well over a hundred years.

Forager's Pot Pie

CRUST

1¼ cups ivory wheat or organic all-purpose flour

1 teaspoon raw turbinado sugar

¼ teaspoon salt

½ cup cold butter, cut into ½-inch pieces

5 tablespoons ice water

FILLING

4 carrots

½ stalk celery

½ bulb fennel

3 to 5 white potatoes

1 red onion

¼ cup morel mushrooms

¼ cup crimini mushrooms

¼ cup shiitake mushrooms

2 cloves garlic

1 tablespoon butter, plus butter for the pie pan

2 tablespoons arrowroot powder

3 cups vegetable stock (or replace 1 cup of stock with 1 cup of whole milk)

1 cup bean sprouts

Mini bouquet of fresh oregano or foraged purslane

¼ cup curly parsley

1 cup corn

Salt and black pepper

Cumin, cloves, or cinnamon (optional)

After we've had a full day of running or exploring in the outdoor air on a fall or winter day, there's nothing quite like serving a steaming hot pot pie to my family for dinner. It feels like dessert the way it's presented, yet it has an incredibly humble essence about it. Its understated warmth and nourishment draw me to this dish, and I am always intrigued with the way the creamy vegetables drip out the side of the warm, buttery crust!

FOR THE CRUST: In a bowl, mix the flour, sugar, and salt. Pinch off sections of the butter and add to the dry ingredients. Carefully sprinkle in the cold water. Mix to combine thoroughly. Form into a ball and wrap the dough in recycled plastic; refrigerate for 1 to 2 hours before use, or toss in the freezer while you prepare the main portion of the pie!

Preheat the oven to 425°F.

Chop the carrots, celery, fennel, potatoes, onion, mushrooms, and garlic. In a large pot, over low to medium heat, melt the butter and add the arrowroot powder and vegetable stock. Whisk until combined, then add in the chopped vegetables and sprouted beans.

Chop the oregano and parsley in fine pieces and set aside.

Allow the vegetables to soften to your liking. I've noticed such variation in what others prefer in regard to this! Some crave a firm, almost crunchiness to their vegetables, and others prefer a soft, almost spongy consistency. Explore here!

Butter a pie pan. Take the crust out of the refrigerator or freezer, and gently roll out into a circle on top of a floured counter. The crust should just extend out from the sides of the pie pan about a ¼ inch or so to create enough space to roll it over less than ¼ inch.

Pour the stovetop contents into the bottom of the pie pan, then add in the fresh corn and chopped oregano and parsley. Season to your liking with basic salt and pepper, a dash of cumin, or a dash of cloves and cinnamon.

recipe continues

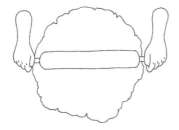

Lay the crust over the top of the pan. Starting on one side, twist the crust inward toward the center of the pie, folding each section slowly and carefully like a continual twist around the edge of the pie. With a toothpick or tip of a butter knife, poke holes evenly on the top of the crust for circulation and even baking.

Bake for 35 to 40 minutes or until the crust is slightly browned and just nearly crisp. I am all about having extra butter nearby to brush on the warm, steaming crust when I serve to my family and others.

NOTE: Most co-ops sell sprouted beans in bulk that are ready to use, but any kind of bean will be delectable here. My favorite alternatives are great white northern or black beans.

Artistry Meets Allergy

I am 7 years old when I gather my bounty of wild, yellow petals and stems. A bouquet so big, I have to wrap both of my pale arms around it to transport it through the painted robin's egg blue front door of my house. I'm attempting to peek through the bouquet to see where I am walking. I run into the door anyway, but the bouquet is brilliant.

I bring it inside and open up the small cabinet of vases that my mom collects. She always had so many of the exact same clear-glass color, yet so many different sizes. Why were there always so many vases? I choose the biggest one, because, well, this bouquet was enormous, you see. (Or at least it was to me back then.) I place the stems inside ever so carefully and intentionally. Finished. It looks so good and I am actually smiling to myself. I leave it on the counter for my family to see. A few hours later, my mom was scooting around in the kitchen, as she always did, and my dad arrived home from work early. I love when this happened. They smiled at me ever so tenderly, and my mom finally got down to my level and basically said, "Sweet girl, you brought in a bunch of terrible weeds that your dad is wildly allergic to." I can actually remember the way he was sneezing and sniffling almost immediately after walking through the blue door but still tender-hearted and thoughtful, to not throw the bouquet away right away. He's like that. My mom and I immediately took the weeds back outside and gathered up the spiders and bugs that accompanied my most delightful agglomeration of earth-grown goods crawling all over her counter. You see, it's all about perspective. One person's eyes will see pure wonder and yet another has an allergic reaction. But the fact is, our perspective is everything. Our mind-set drives our attachments and our actions and ability to appreciate and celebrate someone or something. Surprisingly enough, my dad was the one who showed me what it meant to appreciate something on such deep levels. His eyes were always filled with gratitude for experiences and beauty. And my mom taught me so much, including how to survive in a disheartening world.

The Mighty Mushroom Meat Loaf

1 pound ground beef or ground bison

1 cup chopped in-season mushrooms

½ small purple onion

2 slices whole wheat or spelt bread

1 tablespoon Heirloom Homemade Ketchup (see page 232)

1 tablespoon Spicy Homemade Mustard (see page 83)

1 teaspoon alder smoked salt

1 teaspoon cracked pepper

1 tablespoon turmeric

¼ cup brown sugar (optional)

1 egg

½ cup milk

Fresh raw mushrooms, chopped

Warm. Total comfort, hug-from-Grandma–type vibes. After a chilly or wet hike in the woods, this is an amazing dish to combine all in one bowl and bake for an hour while the wet clothes are exchanged for dry, warm ones. Wool socks are pulled up tight and blankets are gathered. If consumed posthike, it is best eaten curled up under a blanket, in front of an indoor fire, or right on the living room floor for a family picnic experience. This recipe could be made in your sleep, so for all the nights that you feel smothered by "what are we going to make for dinner again?" this mighty mushroom meat loaf is the answer. I absolutely adore a glass of spicy Malbec with this meal.

Preheat the oven to 350°F.

In a skillet over medium heat, sizzle the beef until thoroughly cooked. While that is cooking, chop the mushrooms and onion, tear the bread apart into small sections as if you were feeding the birds with it, and place them into a bowl along with the ketchup, mustard, salt, pepper, turmeric, and brown sugar. Crack open the egg and add it to the mixture along with the milk.

Take the meat off the stovetop and let it cool for a bit. Once the meat is slightly cooled, mix it into the bowl and combine it all by hand. I guess you could use a fork, too, but it won't combine the way that it does if you use your hands.

Bake in a round pie pan or a small bread loaf pan for 1 hour. Check in toward the end, looking for a slightly browned top. Cut in sections and serve! For an additional delight, once each piece has been cut, spread a slice of gouda or bleu cheese on top and watch it melt as you take it over to the indoor picnic area to warm up with.

This simple meal can be paired with greens for a well-rounded and easy dinner. Top with fresh raw mushrooms.

VEGAN ALTERNATIVE: Exchange the beef with 2 cups of mashed beans and replace the egg and milk with ¾ cup vegan butter.

Smokey Bear's Amaranth Black Bean Clover Burger

SMOKEY BEAR SPREAD

2 soft avocados

1 tablespoon maple syrup

$1/4$ teaspoon cayenne pepper

$1/4$ teaspoon cumin

BURGERS

2 cups water

1 cup amaranth grain

1 cup black beans, softened in water (or 15-ounce can, drained)

1 cup wild red clover or dandelions

1 tablespoon olive oil, divided (or oil of choice)

1 fresh, firm tomato, sliced

1 cup fresh sprouts

4 to 6 slices whole wheat bread or sprouted buns

Fresh tomato slices

"Remember, only you can prevent forest fires."

—Smokey Bear

Smokey Bear seemed so earth-grown and intentional with his interactions with the forest, didn't he? I mean his message was so clear: We need to take care of these woods. Cheers to you, Smokey, this burger is for you.

Wild red clovers are rich in protein and make an excellent addition to a cooked meal. Additionally, the flower heads can be dried and steeped for tea, sprinkled on salads, or processed for flour.

FOR THE SPREAD: Combine the avocados, maple syrup, cayenne pepper, and cumin. Set aside.

FOR THE BURGERS: In a medium pot, bring the water to a boil and pour in the amaranth grain. Turn down to medium heat and cover to let simmer. Crush and smash the beans in a bowl, with a fork, to make a puree. Chop the heads of the red clovers or dandelions into edible bites like you would for an herb.

After 15 to 20 minutes, the grain should be close to done. Take a peek to see if the liquid has been absorbed by the grain. If so, turn the heat off and let cool. Once cooled slightly, combine the grain, beans, clovers or dandelions, and $1/2$ tablespoon of the oil and form into disklike shapes to make 4 to 6 burgers.

In a skillet, add the other $1/2$ tablespoon of oil and cook the burgers on high heat to sizzle both sides of the burgers.

Top the burgers with fresh sprouts, fresh tomato slices, and Smokey Bear Spread! Layer between two bread slices or buns or eat fresh with a fork.

Alice in Wonderland Feast

10 purple, orange, and yellow carrots, unpeeled

5 to 7 potatoes, unpeeled

1 head broccoli

1 large red onion

Mini bouquet of fresh oregano

½ cup fresh or dried chopped morels

Chicken breast or beef chuck roast (optional)

3 tablespoons olive oil

½ stick butter

2 cups water

3 bags chamomile tea

3 tablespoons dried chamomile flowers

1 cup whole shiitake mushrooms

I'm certain I will miss playing and acting with my girls someday, but for now I will gladly be the mom who acts out scenes whenever I can. To be a part of their world with the smallest acts can mean so much to little ones. For us to weave into their world of imagination and play is beyond essential. It can shape their minds into being open to new experiences and can communicate a connection to playfulness in an all too serious world.

This recipe is nourishing and magical. I hope Alice would be proud. Curious colors and shapes are the theme here! We seek to eat well because I know it actually affects us all so much. Our mood, emotions, can't-get-off-the-couch syndrome, anxiety—all of these can be affected by what we are actually fueling and feeding our bodies with. An interesting experiment is to track your child's emotional outbursts or frustrations, then go backward to what they ate—how much sugar was tucked in that fruit rollup, how much food coloring is in their system, how their body is reacting to these substances. Calculating the weight of digesting an entire carb-loaded substance can help you recognize that it might be all connected.

If you're drawn to it, try exploring with dried foraged mushrooms. They are an amazing ingredient to use through the winter months. They're bound to make any feast a little more magical. Tuck them in foods with onions, purple carrots, fresh oregano, dried chamomile flowers, and a side of rice. It takes practice to change a child's cravings or habits. They might not like them the first time, but maybe the second or third. Nourishing and magical and so, so easy. Current offerings at most co-ops are dried chanterelles, cremini, lobster, morel, matsutake, maitake, oyster, portabella, porcini, and shiitake. Many mushrooms are incredible sources of selenium, an antioxidant mineral, at levels literally as high as carrots, peppers, tomatoes, and green beans. Truly magical. They provide protein, vitamin C, and an incredible source of iron. They can benefit bone health by adding strength to the teeth, hair, nails, and skeletal system. Plus, you can say you are having Alice in Wonderland stew for supper and maybe it will add a little intrigue and wonder to their small little worlds.

Preheat the oven to 450°F. Line a large rectangular pan with parchment paper. Chop the carrots in half, the potatoes into fourths, the broccoli and the large onion in small sections and distribute them in the pan. Chop the oregano finely and sprinkle on top. Add the dried morels, tucking them in and noting their shape and texture and petite size. Spread the vegetables and fungi apart and place your meat in the center, if desired, then cover it with the earth-grown goods. Drizzle the olive oil over everything and pinch off sections of butter to dot over the entire meal. The butter will melt and drip and dollop!

Bring 2 cups of water to a boil, then turn off the heat, and steep the chamomile tea for 10 minutes. Remove the tea bags and pour the tea over everything. Sprinkle on the dried chamomile flowers.

I don't suggest baking with aluminum foil, so use another layer of parchment paper to cover the top; otherwise place a flat baking sheet over the long, rectangular pan to help contain the moisture. Bake for 40 minutes or until the vegetables fork open easily. Serve with rice or a buttered quinoa side dish.

A Lovage Rosemary Broth with Wildcrafted Frankincense Tears

6 sprigs of rosemary

6 cups water

1 cup chopped fresh lovage

3 cloves garlic, crushed and chopped

¼ teaspoon salt

3 frankincense tears

Dash of apple cider vinegar

I am so drawn to the simplicity of this meal. It's a loosely formed broth soup that is an interesting appetizer for guests as it begins conversations of curiosity and interest. Frankincense tears, when resting in my hand, are a milky white color and crystallized in form. They are firm in texture like rocks found by the river. To appreciate their harvest, the sap is extracted from the tree bark of *Boswellia sacra*, allowed to harden into a gum resin for several days, and then scraped off in tear-shaped droplets. These can be found many herbal stores or ordered online through reputable sources; co-ops in my area have started to sell them as well.

This feels similar to a bone broth to me. Warm and nourishing and light to sip on. It makes an excellent base for many different types of broth journeys.

Peel the rosemary leaves away from the stem and chop into fine pieces. Bring the water to a boil and add the chopped rosemary, lovage, garlic, salt, frankincense tears, and apple cider vinegar. If you are drawn to more of a kick of flavor, visit the bulk section for nourishing broth powders or experiment with your own powdered herbs.

Mulberry Baked Olive'd Carrots

3 pounds rainbow carrots

1 cup lemon oil

½ cup raw walnuts

½ cup pitted whole black olives

½ cup pitted whole castelvetrano olives

1 cup foraged mulberries

1 cup blackberries

½ cup pumpkin seeds

½ cup whole blanched raw almonds

½ fresh lemon

2 tablespoons black salt

Mulberry trees bloom from May through June and grow in many places including small town neighborhoods and cities; one can even be planted in your front yard for seasonal foraging. The fruit is incredibly sweet and when picked barefoot, the fallen ones squish underfoot and stain your feet and hands, marking a most memorable summer experience and connection with the earth. Ripe berries can be shades of white, purple, or reddish brown. They are lovely and calming to pick berry by berry, but one can also lay out a blanket or tarp and gently shake the branches to collect them in a more "bulk" type fashion! Think mulberry pie, mulberry cocktails, mulberry syrup, mulberry jams, mulberry salads, mulberry tacos, or mulberry handfuls. Be forewarned that their unripe fruit and raw shoots contain hallucinogens.

Black salt has become more widely available at many co-ops. It is a most scrumptious salt that adds incredibly unique flavor and is infused with activated black charcoal and essential minerals. It adds depth, complexity, and a cleansing base of black crystals. Magical!

Baked nuts and olives pair so well together in this dish and connect with the baked berries for a perfect blend of salty and sweet. I absolutely love serving this and studying who is drawn to the salty and who is drawn to the sweet.

Wash the carrots with cold water. Cut off the ends but leave them unpeeled. On a large rectangular sheet pan, lay them in lines forming a pattern of your choosing. Notice the beauty of each carrot and how different they are in length and color. Consider how amazing that while many earth-grown goods blossom above the earth's surface, these carrots expanded down inside the earth's dirt, then were lifted up gently to make their way to our plate. If you have carrots with extensive girth (bigger than the size of a quarter), be sure to slice them once in half to open up their center toward the sky.

Preheat the oven to 375°F.

Brush or drizzle the lemon oil over the carrots. With your hands, roll them back and forth, covering them completely in oil. If lemon oil is not available in your area, opt for olive oil in its place and squeeze over the carrots an additional $\frac{1}{2}$ lemon.

Chop the walnuts into fourths, making the sections large enough to fork up easily. Cut the pitted olives into halves. Sprinkle on the walnuts, olives, mulberries, blackberries, pumpkin seeds, and almonds. Squeeze a half lemon over all, letting it drip in and out of everything. Dust with the salt.

Bake for 40 to 55 minutes, checking your carrots for preferred softness! Most people will appreciate a slightly "soft to the fork" carrot consistency, but one must be open-minded!

"Feet on the earth.
Hands in the dirt.
Heart wide open.
Head in the clouds."

Bean and Blossoming Citrus Salad

¼ cup great northern beans, dry or canned

¼ cup black beans, dry or canned

¼ cup black-eyed peas, dry or canned

¼ cup cranberry beans, dry or canned

1 tablespoon olive oil

Seasonings of choice— cajun, cinnamon, and a dash of brown sugar; maple syrup, anise powder, cumin, a dash of celery, garlic, and herb salts; or applewood smoked sea salt

Bouquet of kale

Mini bouquet of fresh leaf lettuce or arugula

2 oranges

2 blood oranges

1 grapefruit

2 tablespoons butter (or more olive oil)

Handful of dried cranberries

This meal could quite literally be made 7 days a week and be an entirely new experience based on the seasoning chosen! There will be leftover greens from this recipe that can be used for lunch the next day. Double the beans and prepare for the next day or if you're in a rush, opt for canned organic beans to top! All beans can be prepared with an overnight sprout and soak or used from a can. Opt for what you are most drawn to in terms of accessibility and time.

On the stovetop over low to medium heat, put the beans into a pot and add the olive oil. Season the beans with the seasonings of your choice: cajun, cinnamon, and a dash of brown sugar; maple syrup, anise powder, cumin, a dash each of celery, garlic, and herb salts; or applewood smoked sea salt. Simmer the beans until they are hot and soft and there is a slight bubbling around the inside edges of the pot.

While the beans simmer, prepare the greens and citrus. Tear apart the kale and the lettuce into smaller sections. Cover an entire plate with the greens almost dripping over the side! Peel the oranges, blood oranges, and grapefruit; with a serrated knife, slice into them into small edible squares. Set them aside.

Once the beans are fully cooked, turn the stove off and add in about 2 tablespoons of creamy butter. Stir and let cool. Spoon the flavorful beans onto the greens and top with the citrus fruit and dried cranberries.

Forager's Fungi'd Campfire Corndogs

1 cup Bob's Red Mill
Paleo Baking Flour
(a blend of almond flour,
arrowroot starch, organic
coconut flour, and
tapioca flour)

¼ cup cornmeal

¼ teaspoon salt

4 teaspoons baking
powder

1 egg

1 cup whole milk

¼ cup butter, softened

Pinch of dry active yeast

¼ cup raw turbinado
sugar

Pinch of nutmeg

½ cup chopped in-season
or dried mushrooms

6 organic beef hot dogs

6 long, wooden kabob
sticks

Pepperjack or cheddar
cheese, chopped raw
mushrooms, or chopped
onions

The way the stars glisten. The sound of darkness. The song of the bugs at night. Staying up past bedtime. The glow from the bright hot fire and the way it draws everyone close to it on a chilly evening. Nowhere to be, but experiencing nature outdoors. Tucked into blankets and curled on laps. The sparks fly upward, mirroring lightning bugs. The calming, repetitive motion of layering on fresh wood and observing the way the fire calms and quiets as it turns into cold coals. To watch a fire all the way to its final glow.

Turn these buttery beef delights over a flame, like one does to warm the front and back of their body, alternating back and forth until evenly baked. With a little bit of preparation ahead of time, these turn out to be quite the addition to a family or friends gathering and offer an activity to engage with around the campfire!

An hour ahead of time, combine the paleo flour, cornmeal, salt, baking powder, egg, milk, butter, yeast, sugar, nutmeg, and chopped in-season or dried mushrooms. Mix until thoroughly combined. Knead like a bread dough, removing any air bubbles! Roll out flat into a rectangle less than a quarter of an inch thick. Fold into thirds. Wrap in recycled plastic and refrigerate for an hour. Take out and roll out into a rectangle about 11 by 13 inches on a floured counter. Then slice into sixths, imagining rectangular shapes, one for each of the dogs. Separate the sections and roll them out, one by one, a little bit thinner, maintaining a rectangular shape. Stack these up with parchment paper in between each.

Use a kabob stick to secure each hot dog. When ready to use, take the hot dog on a stick, and lay it in the center of the dough. Before closing up, tuck in cheese, finely chopped raw mushrooms, or onions and then fold them all in like a blanket, tucking and pinching and giving each a tender roll. Repeat for all.

Cook over an open fire, turning ever so slowly!

Cattail Venison Bouquets

3 tablespoons duck fat oil

1 pound venison steak
(or ground venison with
pepper, cumin, and salt)

1 cup cattail shoots

3 cloves Preserved Garlic
(see page 241)

1 red pepper

2 small tart green apples

Small bouquet of fresh
kale, torn into small
pieces

1 heirloom tomato,
chopped

4 to 6 sprouted grain
tortillas

8 ounces brie cheese,
thinly sliced

So many winters were spent curled up in a wooden A-frame cabin up north with all my cousins. I can close my eyes and feel the way the sleeping bag wrapped me at night up in the top bunk bed, nestled next to my younger sister. The ceiling was worn, with cracks that I followed with my eyes for as far as I could see. The space felt lived in. The days were filled with sledding down seemingly colossal hills, holding on tight for dear life, scream-ing the entire way. The dads would deer-hunt all day while the moms cooked meals. We played games, and my aunts would pay us a mere 25 cents per 10-minute back rub. What a rip-off! It was bliss, though.

The vision behind these venison bouquets is to prepare an overflowingly bountiful bouquet-ed burrito. The sprouted grain tortillas are made from organic sprouted whole wheat, organic un-hulled sesame seeds, organic sprouted whole soy-beans, organic sprouted whole barley, organic sprouted whole millet, organic sprouted whole lentils, organic sprouted whole spelt, and sea salt. They are layered with perfectly cooked ven-ison strips, cattails, caramelized red peppers, tart apples, warm melted brie, tomatoes, red pepper, and fresh kale.

Every single part of the cattail is edible. If you are stranded in the wild, the cattail not only can serve as shelter but can nourish you no matter what season it is.

Cattails can be found in shallow marshes or shallow water and can be used in salads and stews or pickled and fried. In early spring, their shoots can be harvested and eaten raw or cooked similar to asparagus. Through early summer, the flower exudes a bright yellow pollen that can be gathered by gently shaking the branch into a bag and sifted through to use as a cattail flour or thickening agent. Come fall and winter, the starchy centers of the roots can be dried out and used as a flour or thickening agent and, of course, all year long, the cattails can be used for shelter and as a base for imaginative play and wonder!

In a skillet over medium heat, add the duck fat oil and watch the way it slowly spreads out on the pan, preparing itself to soak into the folds of the meat. Venison is a very lean meat, so adding in an additional source of fat will increase the flavor substantially. Slice the venison into thin, elongated strips. Sizzle and flip back and forth until browned on both sides and slightly pink on the inside. Wild game is incredible just slightly undercooked. Set aside.

Chop the cattail shoots and set them into a bowl. Crush and mince the garlic into small portions and toss them into the bowl as well! Chop the red pepper into small sections. Toss in the bowl. Chop the tart apple for variation and a dash of zest and interest and combine in the bowl along with the kale and tomato. Lay thin slices of brie down on each tortilla before adding the meat. Top with a spoonful of the mixed ingredients. Roll up and enjoy!

Cattails

Welcome, Summer. This is the season when the uses for cattail are most abundant. Once a stem is pulled from the ground, you will notice the lower part is white. When eaten raw, it tastes similar to cucumber. Cooked, it tastes like corn. Lower cattail stalks are a good source of vitamins A, B, and C along with potassium and phosphorus. During midsummer, a yellow pollen appears that can be used as flour or a thickener for soups and stews. To harvest the pollen, bend the cattail head into a paper bag and shake. In late summer, green flower spikes appear and can be eaten like corn on the cob!

Hello, Autumn. The root of cattail can now be harvested. Wash thoroughly and submerge in water. Let it sit until a gel forms. Drain the gel and use for making bread and soups. For a protein-rich flour, dry the roots and grind. They can also be roasted and ground for a healthy coffee substitute.

I see you, Winter. In northern climates, cattail root is difficult to collect, but not impossible if you can break through frozen ground and ice. In late winter, new shoots begin to emerge, once again ready to provide a food source.

Exploring and engaging with the world at night becomes magical by dripping a cattail head in oil or fat and using it as a torch to light the way through the woods. The pollen and the cobs are by far the safest and easiest parts to collect. They provide a safe haven for many fish underwater as well as for birds and animals on land. Cattails are quite useful for basket weaving, mat making, or stuffing pillows with their bounty of fluffy pollen.

Growing cattails in pots is doable no matter where you live. Begin by transplanting the cattail seedlings into individual 4-inch greenhouse pots filled with moist, fast-draining soil. Grow them in part shade for 1 to 2 months. Provide 1 to 2 inches of water each week. Increase watering slightly if the weather is very hot and dry. Harvest as shoots begin to blossom.

Sweet Root Maple Chili

½ stalk celery

7 to 9 carrots

2 sprigs of rosemary

½ cup coconut oil

2 cups canned white northern beans, drained

2 cups chili beans

2 cups canned sweet corn, drained

2 cans crushed tomatoes or 5 to 7 heirloom tomatoes boiled down

1½ cups fresh maple syrup

½ cup coconut or brown sugar

3 cups water

3 tablespoons chili powder

1 tablespoon cayenne pepper

1 tablespoon cumin

Dash of black pepper

1½ cups chopped foraged in-season mushrooms (forest nameko make excellent ones)

TOPPINGS

Fresh rosemary, cut into small pieces

Honey goat cheese

This sweet chili pairs well with sap from a freshly tapped spring maple tree. The sap is boiled down and turned into syrup, then melted and mixed with the root vegetables and beans to welcome any sort of cloudy or rainy spring day. It offers variation on the table next to a pot of Deep, Dark Venison Chili (see page 122) with its hints of brown sugar and molasses. It is so good, it can be devoured chilled even in the heat of a summer day.

Begin by chopping the celery, carrots, and rosemary into small, edible bites. Heat up the coconut oil over medium heat, and add them to caramelize and soften. Once they are slightly browned and mostly soft, add in the beans, corn, tomatoes, maple syrup, coconut or brown sugar, water, chili powder, cayenne pepper, cumin, and black pepper. Simmer on low to medium heat, stirring occasionally. At the very end, add in the chopped mushrooms. Serve hot with fresh raw chopped rosemary and honey goat cheese on top.

VARIATIONS include adding cooked ground turkey or tofu. For a thicker end result to use as a topping for sweet chili dogs, skip the water and be sure to drain all of the beans.

Baked Cinderella Pumpkin Soup

2 large Cinderella pumpkins

Olive oil

Butter

6 cups vegetable stock

2 medium-size onions

2 cups foraged acorns or chestnuts

2 teaspoons nutmeg

1 teaspoon cinnamon

¼ cup maple syrup, plus more for serving

10 ounces plain goat cheese, plus more for serving

Pinches of salt and black pepper

3 sweet apples, unpeeled

Bouquet of sage, chopped

1 cup almond milk

TOPPINGS

Baked bacon chunks

Chopped jalapeño

I daydream of backyard pumpkin patches. Opening up the squeaky back door, the same one that lets in just a tiny bit of air through the winter (we seriously have to fix that), I dream of walking out to see lines and rows and small bursts of circles of orange, vibrant green folded leaves, and curled-up stems like ribbon freshly pulled off a spool. I dream of fall picnics in the pumpkin patch on top of a blanket with the girls and their friends. The night before, I would quick-boil and soak some gathered acorns and make something with their tender interior meat. I'd wonder what we'd make for dinner that night and walk out back, barefoot, with my clipper tossing around in my apron pocket, and slice off the fattened stem ever so slowly. Despite a full summer of heat behind me, my arms are still pale as they wrap around the plump and firm circumference of the pumpkin. I would bring it inside the kitchen to prepare and yell something like, "Who wants Cinderella Stew for supper?" The girls scream "Me! Yes! Don't forget the acorns, Mom!" as they run up to me and hug my knees.

The girls set the table and the Bear joins us as I ladle out soup for each of them and sprinkle crushed pumpkin seeds on top, dollop fresh leaf sage, and sprinkle a few pinches of fresh chilled goat cheese. They devour it and say, "Let us do the dishes tonight, Mom! You just lie on the couch, and we will take care of it all!" Remember, this is a dream.

Taking your knife, cut open the top of the pumpkins. Lift the stemmed handle up and notice the stringy and fibrous layers of threads that drip off the top of it. Scoop out the seeds with your hands and gather the clusters of thick wet stringlike scoops, setting them aside to bake. Separate and wash the seeds.

Preheat the oven to 375°F.

recipe continues

Roll each pumpkin on its side, and slice a thin layer off the bottom to leave as much of the "meat" as possible. Chop each into six sections so they will lie flat on a sheet pan. Sprinkle the washed seeds onto the pan. Drizzle the pumpkin sections and seeds with olive oil and butter. Bake for 40 minutes, until the flesh is soft and easy to fork and separate.

Meanwhile, chop and sear the onions on medium heat with a dash of olive oil in a big pot. Peel open the acorns and sizzle the meat inside the acorns with the onions. Let them caramelize just slightly. Add stock to the pot.

Once the pumpkins are baked, take all the meat from the skin and place the soft pumpkin into a food processor or blender and puree. Spoon the contents into the big pot and add more butter and olive oil plus the nutmeg, cinnamon, maple syrup, goat cheese, and pinches of salt and pepper. Chop up the three apples and toss them into the pot along with the chopped fresh sage. Pour in the almond milk and simmer for close to 30 minutes on low to medium heat until warmed. Top with the baked pumpkin seeds, more fresh goat cheese, and a drizzle of maple syrup. Read the Cinderella story.

Chamomile Fennel Trout with Arugula Salad

2 local or foraged trout

Salt and black pepper

Bouquet of fresh or dried chamomile, chopped

Bouquet of fresh lavender, chopped

½ stalk fresh fennel

Garlic salt

6 to 8 ounces goat cheese

½ cup olive oil

½ cup raw walnuts

1 cup whole black olives

1 package strawberries

Drizzle of honey (optional)

A summer fennel feast! This became one of our most treasured meals all through summers, and we got into a habit of making it almost once a week on Fridays like a family date night. We would grill outdoors, cooking over a small open fire, or occasionally we would bake in the oven on overly rainy evenings. We would gather around the kitchen island together while I prepped and share thoughts, new ideas, or reflections from the week. The girls bounce in and out of the kitchen on their bikes that somehow flow from indoors to outdoors as a new sort of "normal."

The preparation is the same whether the trout is being baked, grilled, or flamed over a fire! I can't get over my fascination with the way the fork separates the sections of meat! The tenderness and small hot waves climb into the air from each bite, requiring a quick blow for the first few experiences. Such anticipation for the meal cooked and now finally to be devoured. Fennel is incredibly easy to cook with and paired with chamomile and fresh garden lavender creates such a beautiful "from the fresh lakes" feast.

To bake, begin by filleting the trout. What a beautiful species filled with such nutrition as potassium, phosphorus, protein, and healthy fats. Be sure there are no bones that are visible.

Line a baking sheet with parchment paper and add the filleted fish to it. Sprinkle in the salt, pepper, dried or freshly chopped chamomile, and freshly chopped lavender.

I always use the entire fennel—the bulb, the stalks, and the fernlike branches. I lay it down on its side and begin chopping from one side to the other. The stalks make perfect little Os and usually I make one pile of those and then another pile of the white cuts of the bulb. Chopping in all directions to pair down

recipe continues

the fennel into edible bites, take your time and chop as finely as your heart desires. There's a certain soft crunch that occurs when you leave the stalks in bigger Os. Try it out and see if you are drawn to it! Layer the fennel into the bellies of each trout. Sprinkle with garlic salt and more pepper. (If you are serving someone inclined to spice, be sure to sprinkle in a little cayenne and extra pepper for the perfect gentle punch.) Pinch small sections of goat cheese inside the fillet fish to melt into the meat.

Preheat the oven to 375°F.

Drizzle the olive oil over and close up the fillets. They will not be overly full, so they'll be able to cook just fine as closed. Sprinkle the walnuts, olives, and washed whole strawberries next to the belly of the fish and the tail and spread over the sheet pan. The baked berries paired with the juice of the olives and the slight saltiness of the walnuts will leak out over the pan. Cover with an extra sheet pan or parchment paper and rocks at each corner. Bake for 25 to 28 minutes. Check for the fillet to just fall apart.

If it's casual, serve the fillets directly from the pan, offering a spoon to scoop up the walnuts, baked berries, and olives. If hosting others in your home, serve on a decorative tray or wooden cutting board or slowly heat up a square or rectangular himalayan salt block and serve on there to keep hot. This looks gorgeous and will keep the fish warmed! Collect the baked berries, walnuts, and olives and put them in a side bowl with a spoon. Garnish with a drizzle of honey if you'd like! Pair with the Freshly Awakened Salad (see below).

FRESHLY AWAKENED SALAD

Fresh watermelon

Fresh mint leaves

Arugula

Goat cheese

Honey

Cinnamon

Chop the watermelon into squares, the mint leaves into specks, and mix into the arugula. Pinch off balls of goat cheese to layer in. Drizzle with honey and a dash of cinnamon.

Wild Mushroom Stew

½ head cabbage

1 head broccoli

1 red pepper

10 to 15 carrots

5 tablespoons coconut oil

5 ounces fresh ginger root, grated

1 teaspoon ground ginger

4 garlic cloves, chopped

5 cups Basic Mushroom Stock (see page 155)

Salt and black pepper (consider using French grey sea salt)

½ cup arrowroot powder

1 can coconut milk

4 large portobella mushrooms, chopped

2 heaping cups chopped button mushrooms

2 heaping cups chopped in-season foraged mushrooms

TOPPINGS

Brie or honey goat cheese

Heavy black pepper

Chopped raw mushrooms

Fresh parsley

Mushrooms are so mysterious. They grow from the ground in the most curious locations and in the most intriguing directions and colors. In this recipe, I am so drawn to the deep scent of ginger filling the kitchen, but my favorite part of preparing this dish is garnishing it with raw chopped mushrooms. Their root systems channel so deep into the earth and they center the stew's taste. It's such a grounding meal, and I love bringing intention to that thought when I make this. It offers a warmth that nourishes both body and mind.

Fall in love with this process. Take your time cutting these vegetables and appreciate the colors, shapes, and patterns they emit. How can this cabbage even be so vibrant? It will float in this stew like lace. Coconut oil is incredible for increasing energy for your next adventure. It wards off bacteria and infections and fuels your gut. Seek out French grey sea salt, hand-harvested from the pristine Atlantic seawater and worth the simple search in your grocery store! Double this recipe for great go-to leftovers for a warm, comforting lunch tomorrow.

Chop the cabbage, broccoli, and red pepper into thick chunks. Slice the carrots into small half circles. This is a stew so the spoonfuls should be chunky and stocky to add depth to each bite. In a stockpot, over low heat, simmer the cabbage, broccoli, red pepper, and carrots in the coconut oil until the vegetables have hints of caramelization and are slightly soft.

Add the fresh grated ginger to the pot, and simmer for 10 to 15 minutes on a low to medium heat. Add the ground ginger, garlic, mushroom stock, salt, and pepper and simmer on medium for 10 minutes. Add in the arrowroot powder and coconut milk, bring to a boil, stirring occasionally, then turn back to a low simmer. Add the mushrooms to the stew. Simmer on low to medium heat for about 20 minutes.

To serve, top with a soft cheese such as brie or honey goat cheese, heavy amounts of black pepper, raw mushrooms, or fresh parsley.

BASIC MUSHROOM STOCK

3 cups water

1 cup white wine

2 pounds chopped
portobello and button
mushrooms (if foraged,
turkey tail or maitake
mushrooms make excellent
choices to boil down for
broth)

½ cup apple cider vinegar

Pinch of salt

Bring the water, wine, mushrooms, vinegar, and salt to a boil, simmer for 5 minutes, then set the heat back to low. Cook for 30 minutes. Let cool, soak for a few hours, then strain. Use the strained mushrooms for this soup or another dish!

Chapter 5

LIFE IN THE WOODS

Indoor Nature Preservations and Display

Nature preservation is a tangible way to connect with nature. Collect a very small amount of any fallen earth-grown good that you are drawn to. It could be a daisy, a mushroom, a worn leaf, a fern, a feather, or a root. Anything that inspires you might represent an interaction or experience you had that day with the earth. Depending on the moisture level, your nature find can be displayed immediately or otherwise dried in a large book or floral press. Press the item inside the book or floral press and allow to dry and flatten for up to 4 days before displaying.

Display in a glass frame or box and hang it on the wall or rest it on a shelf. Collect used or new frames with the color of your choice. On a nontoxic piece of archival-grade paper, write letters to your kids on the back. Write memories from that day or hopes or dreams or anything you are learning lately. Sketch your ideas, thoughts or designs. Write about why you were drawn to that particular item or where you are in life.

Mushrooms range in moisture level as well and some of them that I've framed have preserved perfectly and others did not. To rid the mushroom of bugs, bacteria, and moisture, put them in the oven for less than 8 minutes at 450°F for a flash bake. This allows them to dry out faster, preserves them longer, and keeps your surfaces clean.

On the front of it, give it a title.

Our First Summer in the Woods

From the Day the Acorn Fell

Fall 2018

Hot, Humid, and Halfway Through Growing a Life

Write anything that your heart desires. Lay the pieces flat and be open to using nontoxic double-sided tape to keep the materials more secure. Take a piece of glass and layer it on top, then add the frame, and flip it over to secure with backing. Hang on the wall with other nature finds to form a growing collection of earth-grown goods. They will be like a time capsule, documenting findings and experiences with nature for years to come.

I began collecting pieces that were meaningful to me and the girls and Max since we moved into the A-frame. At both of our houses, we had a small corner of the room in which we called the Nature Center. We display finds and gathered goods as a tangible way to provoke appreciation, study new shapes and colors and textures, and bring the outdoors in. But it fills up fast. So displaying them on the wall expands the magic in a new form. I dream of one day filling all the walls in our home with nature finds, as if it were a big museum of treasures and memories.

Some of my favorite preservations are the eggshells from the very first duckling that we incubated and hatched in our home one spring and the wildflower crown from the day I did nothing else besides picnic with the girls, make flower crowns together, and read and play with them. Those are the days I hope to remember as their mom—the ones where the house was a mess but our eyes and hearts were connected.

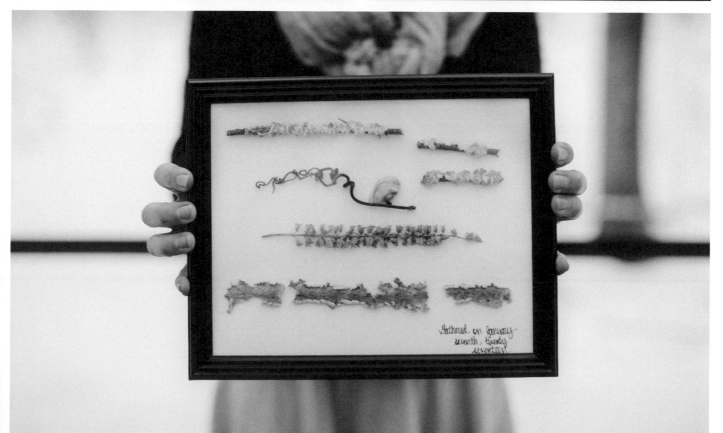

An Ode to Minimalist Footwear

What's the first thing we do after a long day? Generally, one of them is to take our shoes off. There are innate reasons why we follow that tug—it's because our feet were meant to be free. Consider their design. They have 26 bones, 33 joints, in varied sizes and shapes. Actual muscles, like all other muscles in the body, crave to be moved and worked in order to feel their healthiest, function properly, and ultimately allow us to explore the world without pain.

Since I married the Bear, he has downloaded a plethora of knowledge into my brain regarding footwear. Whether it's hiking, climbing, running, walking casually outdoors, or wearing indoor footwear, each of our shoes must pass the minimalist footwear test. The toe of the shoe is bent to the heel of the shoe in an upward motion and must be able to create a "C" shape. The point of it is to prove that the foot will be able to move and function freely as it was designed to do.

Softstar Shoes explains that caring for a child's feet will benefit their health, mobility, and well-being throughout their entire lives. According to the Society of Chiropodists and Podiatrists, the 26 bones in their feet are not fully hardened or ossified until between ages 12 and 18. In fact, children's feet are composed of relatively soft and flexible cartilage that gradually converts to bone with age. While children's feet are developing, the soft cartilage centers are fusing together. As such, the foot is at risk from injury and deformity due to ill-fitting footwear. Any postural foot abnormality can have an effect farther up the body and permanently alter posture, walking style, strength, and coordination.

> Children need full freedom of movement throughout the day in order to develop the body and the senses properly. The feet are no exception. Children greatly benefit from walking barefoot to foster strong and capable feet and to safely navigate their surroundings. When children are required to wear shoes, I highly recommend Vivobarefoot. These shoes allow children to walk in stores, schools, and in other buildings, while still reaping the many benefits of being barefoot. My own daughters have Vivobarefoot and they ADORE them! They are super comfortable and I love that they are also supporting healthy foot development at the same time.
>
> —Angela Hanscom, founder of TimberNook and author of *Balanced and Barefoot*

Barefoot is best for healthy foot development! Obviously it is not always practical to be barefoot, which is why good shoe design is important for warmth and protection while simulating barefoot conditions.

Here are some tips for finding healthy minimalist shoes.

- Wear thin-soled, movable, and bendable shoes.

- Allow plenty of room for toes to wiggle and spread. This means not only in your shoes, but care should also be taken to make sure that socks are loose and sleep suits for children do not cram the toes.

- When buying for children, find soft toddler shoes from reputable companies designed specifically for their age group. Encourage Waldorf or Montessori types of shoe wear. A young child's foot is a different shape from that of an adult or teenager, requiring a correspondingly much bigger toe area than that in an adult shoe. Many shoe manufacturers simply scale down adult shoes to make shoes for children, but this is not recommended.

- Soling material for outdoor shoes on hard surfaces, such as sidewalks, should be slip-resistant, shock-absorbing, low-profile (no heels whatsoever), and flexible with no "molding" features like arch supports.

- The upper portion of shoes should be made of breathable material such as leather or cloth. Hiking, running, walking, casual shoes—whether indoor or outdoors—should be bendable, movable, and thin-soled.

- Go barefoot as often as possible. It's as simple as that! Train your children from age 0 by repeating to them, "Your feet are strong! Your feet are strong!" The hope is that they'll gain a confidence for walking barefoot outdoors while simultaneously strengthening their toes, feet, legs, and body. Luella was running over rocks and pinecones at age 2, completely unphased by it because she had strength in her mind to believe in her feet and built-up barefoot bottoms.

TOP RECOMMENDED MINIMALIST SHOE COMPANIES

Softstar Shoes

Minnetonka Moccasin

Vivo Barefoot

The Magic of Mini

There is a peculiar wonder when things are smaller than they ought to be. Little sisters, little spoons, new puppies, and teeny tiny mushrooms. Everything is more magical when it's mini. Those teeny, tiny, almost too small to hold in a regular human-size hand spoons for salt? Aren't those the best? Simple items like these are everything that's good in the world and not only magical for children, but for adults as well.

I seek out petite mugs that are just the right size for growing hands as well as teeny plates, petite vases, pocket-size jars for miniature finds, itty-bitty bowls for dollops of honey, cute as a button serving spoons and forks—the ones that make you stop and pause and stare at it and say, "Is this real? How adorable!" A breakfast fit for an itsy-bitsy gnome or fairy would always include some sort of mini. It offers a deeper connection to a child's world just by providing space and things that fit them and no longer make them a small child in a big world, but a child in a world that fits them.

SUPPLY LIST FOR A MINI PARTY

Small lace coasters

Miniature straws

Mini salt and pepper shakers

Single egg cast-iron pans

Small tea sets

Mini mugs

Baby acorns and pinecones

Small sections of moss to dry and pull out as decor

Miniature woven baskets

Tiny beeswax candles

Mini muffins

Individual quiches

Bud vases

Acorn caps as cups

Bite-size chocolate chip cookies

Mini-size party hats

A small table and chair set, baby bear style

Mini beer flights

Mini kombucha flights

Gnomes

Fairies

Small gardening tools

Teeny, tiny terra-cotta pots

Forest Fungi

Growing mushrooms at home makes for an incredible winter tabletop project. Based on the mushroom kit, you can grow foragable mushrooms in a matter of weeks. Like a sourdough bread culture, a good strain of mushroom will keep going and going when given the right growing conditions. A mushroom comes and goes—travels, stays for awhile, nourishes other people or other animals or the earth, and then leaves softly and sweetly, like a whisper. I experienced a mammoth-size tree that grew up toward the sky and then back over toward the earth. It had three monstrous mushrooms on it, yet by the next morning they had shriveled down to a miniscule level, having been eaten by deer or some other woodland animal. New ones had grown in, right next to them, bringing new possibilities for the deer walking by. They exist as an aid for the forest environment. There is an actual exchange of nutrients, one providing to the other what it cannot synthesize or extract from the soil by itself. The mushroom helps the tree extract minerals and water from the soil; in exchange, the tree supplies the mushroom with sugar compounds or carbohydrates that it needs for survival and growth. A splendid example of give and take. A cycle that is irrevocably gracious and giving. An exchange of goods.

An oyster mushroom or shiitake log kit can be cared for and harvested right in your own kitchen with little effort and no mess. Logs are hand-cut and inoculated with shiitake mushroom spores in visible drill holes that are covered in cheese wax. They can be stood upright or laid horizontally for growing. All that needs to happen is to simply soak the log for 24 hours in cold water, mist it occasionally, and watch your crop emerge.

If you have land or a front yard and you want to engage with it in a sustainable way, then plant raised garden beds, have fenced-in plots, or raise homegrown fungi—all are ways to connect with the earth.

Fungi Perfecti offers a wide array of indoor growing kits such as Antler Reishi, Blue Oyster, Enokitake Patch, Lions Mane, King Stropharia, Maitake, Mycelium Running Oyster Mushroom Patch, Pioppino, Pearl Oyster, Shiitake, and Turkey Tail! These are all incredibly affordable and clean ways to engage with fungi in the kitchen and wildly tangible ways to connect with the earth. Aside from the practicalities of where you live and how you grow, it's both a doable and beautiful task!

With container growing, one must take into consideration pot size, drainage needs, and indoor access to air and light. Earth-grown goods can be successfully grown in almost any kind of container. When planning for a garden and ordering seeds in the early part of the year, a simple mindfulness toward forest-grown goods will change the bounty that comes from the earth. It will change the way you cook and bake and add an ounce of magic and a bit of wonder into your feast, morning pancake, or even a plate of eggs. Small appreciations.

Worm Composting:
As Good and Gross As It Sounds!

Once upon a time there were two tomato plants. They each had the same bucket, the same soil, the same love song sung to them each morning, and the same sun. The only difference was the water in which they were fed. One drank water and one drank compost tea. Can you guess which one of these plants grew to be four times larger in size? Can you guess which one of these propagated tomatoes grew to be four times larger than the other?

So, why compost? And why worms? Why not just compost in the backyard with food and leaves and leave it at that? And how does one brew compost tea?

Worms are living creatures and play a vital role in the balance of our ecosystem. Worms mix and aerate the soil in the forest, our lawns, and even sections of local city parks, and they increase the nutrients of the land.

Vermicomposting offers a convenient way to dispose of organic waste, such as vegetable peelings, fruit waste, eggshells, and coffee grinds, that accumulates throughout the week. Composting saves space in the county landfill, which is good for the environment. It gives worms a happy home and all the free "eats" that they could want. For those who have gardens or even potted plants, homegrown compost is an incredible way to feed, nurture, and grow plants.

Traditional composting relies solely on microorganisms like bacteria and fungi to break down food particles into new soil. It requires active maintenance so it doesn't stagnate, while in vermiculture, the worms speed up the process for you. Once microbes have taken care of some of the beginning predigestion, the worms take in the food through their mouths. They do not have teeth, but their bodies, which are made of such strong muscles, grind the food into even smaller pieces; they form microbes in their intestines and then complete the digestion, converting the food into nutrient-rich fluid—worm juice. Vermiculture is like normal composting, but completely turbocharged. Incredible. I know.

To find out how large of a compost container you would need for yourself or your family, begin with experimentation. Leave out a large bowl with a top on it on your counter for 2 weeks. Drain the liquids in the sink, but throw all your excess food in this bowl during this time. It will be varied, obviously, based on how often you cook at home and what kind of meals you make. Collect what's left after each meal and each snack and place it in the bowl. Once you've determined your sizing needs, explore local hardware shops for exterior composting tubs or anywhere online by searching for indoor composting options to find what suits your home, space, and needs best.

A general flow for me is to have an interior/exterior compost system. We store all our excess waste in a bowl inside the house that I cover and tuck in the corner under my sink, and then walk it out to the compost once a week. The organization works for me. You can just as easily set up an indoor mini worm compost underneath your sink in a studio apartment, worms and all. If your compost is set up correctly, there should be no smell.

Compost Tea

1 large container (such as an aluminum feeding trough, which is a long, narrow, open receptacle, usually boxlike in shape, used chiefly to hold water or food for animals)

1 bucket of starter black soil or dirt (can be purchased or dug from the earth)

1 bucket of excess leaves

1 family of red wigglers*

1 collection bucket (3- to 5-gallon size)

1 wedge for tilting the compost bin (a brick, a large rock, a cement block . . .)

* We buy our worms from Planet Natural, who sources from an organic worm farmer; their passion is happy, cared-for worms.

Begin by choosing your location for your compost. You want it to be close enough to your home so that you aren't making a long trip out back. The ideal location is a deck or a raised area so that one end of the container can be slightly elevated off the ground on cement blocks or bricks, making it much easier to collect the compost tea.

Flip the container upside-down and drill three to five holes on the bottom side of the bin on one end, like a cluster of stars. This is where your compost tea will drain from. Flip back right-side up and build layers like a smoothie. Start with the soil, then the leaves, then gently pour in the worms. Remember that they are animals, too, and that they have traveled far to come to where you are. They might be exhausted from the journey. I know I would be. Place the collection bucket just below the drilled holes to gather the liquid and magic potion that will inevitably flow from the container.

Repeat the layers: soil, leaves, and then top with the beginnings of your compost—egg shells, banana peels, old watermelon, you name it. Gently mix the contents. We use a stirring log that is about 4 inches thick and 3 feet long but you can use a shovel or rake or really anything. Get your gloved hands in there—that's okay, too. Be brave. Maybe it's a little gross, but definitely doable. Feed and nourish your garden, trees, plants, and flowers with this. Happy worms, happy everything growing.

Unpleasant odors in a worm bin may result from too much food waste, too much moisture, or composting cheese or animal products. Control odors by removing excess waste. You can also make sure that the drainage holes are not blocked or add more drain holes or fresh bedding of soil and leaves if needed. Always cover fresh food waste with at least 1 inch of bedding.

When it gets colder, your worms will slow down and will not be able to digest as much food waste. You will most likely need to cut back on the amount of food waste you feed your worms between November and February. Red worms can survive cold winters outside if protected by bedding in a worm bin.

Worms need oxygen to live. The oxygen diffuses across the moist tissue of their skin, from the region of greater concen-

tration of oxygen (air) to that of lower concentration (inside the worm). Carbon dioxide produced by the bodily processes of the worm also diffuses through skin. Moving from higher concentration to lesser concentration, carbon dioxide moves from the inside of the worm's body out into the surrounding bedding. There should be a constant supply of fresh air throughout the bedding that helps this desirable exchange take place.

Ducklings at the A-Frame

One spring, just a few weeks before Easter, we picked up a brown box of 24 small fertilized duck eggs. They were the prettiest colors—cloudy pale white and slight pale blue. They were a perfect oval shape and each one fit just in the palm of my hand. They felt oversized and slightly warm. A duck egg is generally two-thirds larger than a chicken egg. Their 130 calories far surpass the roughly 70 calories in a chicken egg. Ducks are quieter than chickens, generally healthier, more heat-tolerant, substantially more cold-hardy, richer in flavor, generally less aggressive, and easier on one's lawn and lay eggs more regularly. I did so much reading and research on the incubation process, yet it still made me nervous. It's such a tender and detailed process that spans 28 days.

It was such an inspiring process to view the embryos turn into ducklings, all the while caring for them, surging intention toward their small white box made of plastic and styrofoam, wires, and thermometers. We pulled the eggs out of the styrofoam and took them into the dark bathroom where we "candled" each egg, all four of us cozied up with the lights out. Before electricity, the light from a candle flame was used to check for veins and embryo presence inside of a fertilized egg. I shined a flashlight on the bottom of each egg to search for hairline cracks. We patched a few of the very small ones with a small amount of melted beeswax to prevent bacteria and air from entering through the shell, which was recommended by my farmer friend!

Once the incubator was warmed up to 99.5°F, it was ready to house the eggs. We studied and observed them before placing them into the incubator, resting them gently in their small growing beds. The beds were white and round and warm. We placed the eggs pointy side down. The black wire inside the box was the temperature thermometer and the red wires measured the humidity level. There were small trays or grooves in the bottom of the inside of the incubator that served as water channels to increase the humidity inside. General humidity needed to be 80 percent during the incubation process, then needed to rise to 94 percent during the last 5 days of the growing calendar. Ventilation was needed and it was important to be able to offer fresh oxygenated air for the respiration of the developing embryos because oxygen is essential for the first days and increasingly needed as the calendar goes on.

Included was a glass probe thermometer. I placed it on the top of the duck eggs to assure that they stayed at exactly 99.5 degrees and it helped keep the digital thermometer in check. Each day we checked on them through the clear window, the girls sang to them, and some mornings we set up a picnic blanket for breakfast on the floor just to be close by. The month went by quickly. Then one evening, the Bear and I were sitting on the couch talking after the girls had fallen asleep, and we heard a quiet crunching noise from the incubator. I jumped up and peered through the top clear window and sure enough, a duck had made its way through the shell. Its feathers were wet and stringy and glorious! The next day we saw another small crack in an egg, and I sat for close to 10 of the 19 hours it took the duckling to erupt fully from its egg home. We named her Snowflake and she attached to my daughter as her "Mama Duck," which she, of course, was delighted in. It was so beautiful.

There was so much intrigue and patience and care put into the incubating of eggs for the first time. We didn't have quite as many hatch as we had expected, but those that burst from the shell became a part of our family.

Later that month, the girls learned a tough life lesson on the "circle of life" as our teddy bear–like dog got a little too curious and ate up two of the baby chicks. I sat in the front yard grass, holding my oldest daughter tight as we both cried together over Charlotte and Chamomile. It was the most tender and sad day and made me realize how little we were accustomed to circle of life experiences in farm life. The girls grew a little wiser that day and learned a little more about the alternate experiences of life.

As the ducklings grew, they were greeted every morning (and I mean every morning) by Luella, our oldest, as she woke with the sun, got dressed, and went to check on them. Some mornings she would burst in as we were still sleepy-eyed and groggy and give us duck announcements like, "Emergency! One of the ducks flew out of the container! But I put her back!" or "Okay, it's all okay! They are all still sleeping!"

The ducks are now fully grown; they have free range and forage for bugs and plants throughout their days at the A-frame. They greet us when we come home and quite literally run through the sprinkler with the girls on hot summer days.

Family Living

Sunday afternoons creep in and the Bear goes through his workout in the front yard. The girls always want to join him and basically stalk him through the front windows, bombarding the door to try to join him. He finishes, and I let the wild cattle out through the front door, cheering, "Go! Go! Go!" He walks them through a workout. One of the differences that we forgot to anticipate in moving to the woods was the lack of walkable parks. We had to get more creative with physical activity unless we wanted to pack up and drive to a park. Climbing trees, carrying bottles of water, doing exercises all across the front deck like races at a summer camp, taking long hikes, and running with the dogs became our ways of getting their bodies moving and strong. They got quickly used to taking small steps to climb the body of a barked tree trunk and swinging from old deer-stand ropes hanging from trees. With nature as in the playground, the ups and overs and belows of wild sticks and logs and mossed floors became the sand of their playground. My oldest daughter now prefers to walk barefoot on our woods walks.

There wasn't ever a day all winter long that was "too cold" to get outside. Even if for only a small duration, just to experience the negative temperatures on the tips of their noses and cheeks, was worth it. Of course, there are emotions and opinions outdoors, but wildly less than there are inside. I always imagine the front door as the door to Narnia. There can be much frustration when searching for each mitten and layer. The sweat starts to sink into the layers of wool when one sister is ready but the others are not. We finally break through the sparkling entrance into the outer world. Their emotions even out. Their eyes widen. Out here, there isn't anything to fight over, because there are always enough sticks on the ground to offer. There are enough birds for everyone to see. Out here there are no toy messes, squished cereal crumbs, or TV shows to zone out to. There are no dirty plates or crusted egg pans. There's no looking perfectionism. There are no expectations here. The breath inhaled and exhaled is used solely to seek magic and explore the goodness of the earth. The words used are ones chosen to describe objects and textures, instead of complaints. Our eyes are fully open and wide. Our heart rates can't help but be altered to a higher level outdoors, making indoor rest even more pleasurable by contrast. Everything is alive. There are no doors that slam or close. There are no walls. There are soft voices and loud textures. There are other small lives that matter beside our own. There are other ideas that exist beside my own. Passing through that door is like a step out of our own world and into the world of another. There are still babies to be held, messes to be had, and 4-year-olds with opinions, but those are some of the most beautiful things after all.

Before humans took to farming the land, all people were hunter-gatherers. We imploded into nature to hunt wild animals and to gather wild flowers, plants, nuts, berries, and fungi as sustenance. Curiosity, intrigue, and appreciation for the discoveries were innately parts of the culture, for they signified survival. To come across a bouquet of earth-grown goods became a crowning opportunity to feed ourselves and our families with deeply rich and vibrant nutrients. We used to use every muscle in our body to chase after wild game. We would study the land and become one with it.

I imagine that both the eldest and the youngest in a family studied food quite differently than we do now. Because their life was ruled by engaging with an appreciation for earth-grown goods, they interacted with the world in a different way as well. A movable flourishing feast was their everyday life and whether old or young, they chased after it with all that they had. Food was magic and being open to new experiences in the woods was to be alive.

And then, I think, what if we could experience that now. What if food and life are woven much closer than we know. The way we view food could dramatically change the way we view our life. We could take that mind-set to discover, live in wonderment, and earnestly seek the magic of life and bring it to our table to nourish both our bodies and minds and the bodies and minds of others.

Here are some questions to ask in the woods or at a forest-themed dinner party.

If you could be an animal in the forest, what would you be and why?

What does moss smell like? Does moss live through heavy snowfalls and winter?

Describe a childhood memory that connects you with nature.

Describe the best you have ever felt outdoors?

When's the last time you've made love under the stars? Would you do that?

Describe yourself. You are a mushroom. Where do you grow from and what do you look like?

You are a season. Describe which one you are.

What do you love most about a freezing rain?

Describe your ultimate snowball size and balling technique. What tips would you give to a 7-year-old, just before a snowball fight?

What's the first pollen a bee feeds on in springtime?

How many types of pine can you name?

How many types of fungi can you name?

Tell me a made-up story about a bird.

Tell me a made-up story about a feather.

When you listen to the wind, what do you hear?

Would you eat fresh rose petals? Please say yes.

Lilac in the spring smells like . . .

We try to eat well because I know it affects us all so much. Our mood, emotions, can't-get-off-the-couch syndrome, anxiety—all of these can be affected by what we are actually fueling and feeding our bodies with. An interesting experiment is to track your child's emotional outbursts or frustrations, then go backward . . . what did they eat, how much sugar was tucked in that fruit rollup, how much food coloring is currently in their system, how is their body reacting to these substances or to the weight of digesting an entire carb-loaded meal? So if you're in a postholiday cooking rut, try exploring with foraged mushrooms. They are an amazing ingredient to use through the winter months. They're bound to make any feast a little more magical. Tuck them in with roasted onions, purple carrots, fresh oregano, dried chamomile flowers, and a side of rice. It takes practice to change a child's cravings or habits. They might not like it the first time, but maybe the second or third. Nourishing and magical and so, so easy. Current offerings at most co-ops are dried chanterelles, crimini, lobster, morel, matsutake, maitake, oyster, portabella, porcini, and shiitake. Many mushrooms are incredible sources of selenium, an antioxidant mineral; they provide as much as carrots, peppers, tomatoes, and green beans. Truly magical. They provide protein, vitamin C, and iron. They can benefit bone health by adding strength to the teeth, hair, nails, and the skeletal system. Plus, you can say you are having Alice in Wonderland stew for supper and maybe it will put a little intrigue and wonder into their small little worlds.

Meditation with Kids

When we first moved into the A-frame, we started a weekly family meditation time. The same day of the week, same rectangle carpet squares, same humans. It felt like we were experiencing a lot of change—moving into a new house is a lot to take in for a little one. It was a simple way to reconnect as a family and share our hearts, apologize if needed, start fresh, talk about intentions, and share what we were grateful for, what we want to work on, while we moved our bodies through stretches or yoga. We all enjoyed it so much and found that it provided so much value to our family life, to slow down together. So now we do it closer to every day if we can—the carpet squares are torn and worn, and a year later, they definitely needed to be replaced.

There are many ways to incorporate meditation, rest, or slowed activity into a child's world, and I can't express what a difference it's made in our lives and throughout our homeschooling journey as well.

HOW TO MEDITATE WITH KIDS

1. Start small. Don't expect much.

2. Give them a physical space to be on. A blanket, a carpet square, a log, a rock. But don't expect them to stay there and don't shame them if they wander away from that space.

3. Everything stays positive. Draw them back in with a tender voice, an open mind, or a story. Keeping a smile on your face and an open lap or arms lets them know they are welcomed and heard and seen.

4. Find your flow. We begin by going around the circle saying what we are grateful for, what we are excited about. Max and I will take turns asking:

   Are there any worries on anyone's minds?

   What do you want to get better at today?

   What is one thing you are grateful for?

5. Bring a reading or a song—a poem, a verse, a children's story with intention, or a quote.

6. Verbalize mantras. Max always leads us through these, and they are simply phrases we repeat to each other and ourselves. With many things in life, the way we speak to ourselves and our kids becomes the voice in both our heads and theirs. It sets the tone for the morning, the day, and essentially, our life.

   My body is healthy.

   I am grateful to be alive.

   I will love myself and others today.

   I will offer those around me grace and kindness.

7. Bring in physical movement of some kind to either warm up or cool down. Yoga, stretching, expansion of the lungs, or literally jumping up and down until all the wiggles are out, and then sit calmly.

8. Integrate a bell or have your children choose a timer sound on your phone or timer. Start small by telling them that for the next 10 seconds, 25 seconds, 45 seconds, 5 minutes, or 30 minutes, "we will all sit still without talking and our eyes will be closed until we hear the song play." No shame! Let them watch you do it even if they don't want to or can't. Gently welcome them back to their space with a kind smile and voice and a simple "shhh." Listen for the sound. Point to your ears. Smile. Each time you practice, they will get better and better and even if they hate it the first 10 times, number 11 might just be the magic moment.

9. If they scream, "No!" try saying, "That's fine if you don't want to join us. Right now it's quiet time. You are welcome to sit with us when you are ready." Carry on, even if just you having a moment of peace. They are watching regardless.

10. The goal is connection and trust building. The less expectation we have as parents, the greater the results. Guide them in, welcome them, accept them for wherever they are at that day, showing that not only can they trust you, but also that they are enough just the way they are.

We hope to incorporate this into our girls' lives for as many years as we can. I imagine the topic of conversations will change as the years do, but to come together as a family at an intentional time to just exist seems to build a level of trust and openness that we hope to give and have with the girls for the rest of their lives. An "it's okay if you come to your mat angry, sad, excited, or happy. We just want to meet you there."

Chapter 6

BEVERAGES

COCKTAILS

Each one of these cocktails begins with a foraged herb or plant and a honey-based simple syrup. The syrups will each yield about 8 glasses from approximately 13.4 ounces of foraged syrup. The supplementary syrup can be stored away in the fridge for additional cocktails, to top off a simple dessert, to sweeten oatmeal, or to burst life into creamy coffee. Each cocktail can be served strong, over ice, or served light, over sparkling water or tonic water. Explore with your preferences.

The Wolf

½ cup chopped and crushed wolfberries/ goji berries

½ cup chopped and crushed juniper berries

2 cups water

2 cups honey

2 ounces gin

1 ounce St. Germain liqueur

Wolfberries lead two lives. They are incredibly nutritious yet wildly invasive. Their fruit tastes like a blend between cranberries and the spiciness of anise. Their tender leaves are edible as well and offer a pleasant hint of bitterness of an apple. The wolfberry, commonly called goji berry, tolerates intense amounts of heat and is completely self-pollinating.

There are more than 60 species of juniper to be found and foraged all over the world. Their berries can be harvested midsummer to late fall when they turn a reddish orange hue. When paired with wolfberries and St. Germain, which has hints of elderflower, they make a sweet yet earthy drink that feels summery but sophisticated.

In a saucepan, combine the wolfberries and juniper berries with the water and honey. Cook on low heat until the honey is dissolved. Bring to roaring boil for about a minute to allow it to thicken. Then turn off the heat and set aside to cool. Strain the berries. Store in an airtight jar or container.

When ready to serve, mix the gin, St. Germain, and ½ ounce foraged syrup in a pitcher and pour individual portions over ice. Or engage with a lighter option and mix each drink with 2 ounces sparkling water and ice.

The Sloth

1 cup clean fresh or
dried chamomile flowers
and leaves

1 cup clean calendula
flowers

2 cups water

2 cups honey

2 ounces tequila

A sloth is everything that's hilarious and amazing in this world. Beyond chill. The only time he leaves his tree home is to go to the bathroom, which is roughly once a week, and he occasionally integrates a quick swim before heading back up to eat. Sloths sleep as long as humans do, around 8 or 9 hours, but otherwise they make no conscious attempt to be social or friendly with others. And you know what? That's amazing. Everyone needs that once in awhile. He eats whatever is in front of him, gets his necessary water intake from his food, and takes more than a month to digest his meal. When we make this drink, we embody the sloth and embrace all things cozy. This cocktail is a self-acclaimed, embracing-all-the-homebody-vibes type cocktail.

In a saucepan, combine the chamomile flowers and leaves and calendula flowers with the water and honey. Cook on low heat until the honey is dissolved. Bring to boil for about a minute to allow it to thicken. Then turn off the heat and set aside to cool. Strain the flowers and leaves. Store in an airtight jar or container.

When ready to serve, mix the tequila and 1 ounce foraged syrup in a pitcher and pour individual portions over ice. A lighter option is to mix each drink with 2 ounces sparkling water and ice.

The Red Tree Vole

2 heaping cups foraged
pine tips

2 cups water

2 cups honey

1½ ounces vodka

1 small lime or
1 ounce lime juice

1 orange

During spring trees such as pine, cedar, fir, and balsam sprout new blossoming growth buds. They will be less than an inch long, soft and light in color. Excellent to snack on, cook with, and made into a syrup for the perfect woodland cocktail. The soft citrus and earthy flavor makes for one of my favorite cocktails to serve at a gathering, especially when paired with a small sprig of pine shooting out the glass. Be sure to harvest a small amount in an even fashion from the tree branches as to not stunt their growth and to save some for others.

In a saucepan, combine 2 cups foraged and cleaned pine tips with the water and honey. Cook over low heat until the honey is dissolved. Bring to a boil for about 2 minutes to allow it to thicken. Then turn off the heat and set aside to cool. Strain the needles. Store in an airtight jar or container.

Mix the vodka, 1 ounce lime juice, and ¾ ounce foraged syrup in a pitcher and pour individual portions over ice. Slice thin sections of an orange to rest on the edge of the glass with a small bouquet of pine needles or floating, fresh pine tips.

For a warming rainy spring day cocktail, heat 6 ounces water and combine ¾ ounce foraged syrup and 2 ounces bourbon or rum. Stir in ½ teaspoon of honey and steep 1 bag of Earl Grey tea.

The Champagne Bee

2 cups tightly packed
foraged dandelion flowers
or early budding spring
leaves

2 cups water

2 cups honey

2 ounces gin

1 ounce chilled
Champagne

Making peace with the dandelions in your yard reaps more worthy and honorable qualities than you'll know. Bees, beetles, and birds rely upon them for the first nourishment of the spring season, so before you wage war and go ripping them out root by root, notice how they actually aren't that bad to look at. Consider that you just might be extracting from another life. Bumblebees, honeybees, hoverflies, beetles, and birds such as the peacock and holly blue all utilize the nutrition from the lustrous golden bloom! Invested in appearances and worried that your neighbors will think you're just a lazy landscape keeper? Make a homemade sign that says, "Feel the breeze. Save the bees. Don't pick your dandelions, please!"

In a saucepan, combine cleaned dandelion flowers or leaves, depending on which season it is, with the water and honey. Cook on low heat until the honey is dissolved. Bring to roaring boil for about a minute to allow it to thicken. Then turn off the heat and set aside to cool. Strain the petals and leaves. Store in an airtight jar or container.

When ready to serve, mix the gin, Champagne, and 1 ounce foraged syrup in a pitcher and pour individual portions over ice. An alternate option is to combine 2 ounces whiskey and 1 ounce foraged syrup in a pitcher and pour individual portions over ice.

The Red Squirrel

¼ cup cardamom seeds or powder

¼ teaspoon cinnamon, plus more for serving

2 cups water

2 cups honey

2 tablespoons maple syrup, plus more for serving

2 ounces whiskey

The tree dwelling red squirrel is a crafty little thing. When its bundle of nuts and pinecones begins to diminish, the squirrel harvests sap from the maple tree. It scores the bark of the tree, allowing the sap to drip out and dry in the sunshine, and then it revisits the sugar operation to lick it up with its (I can only imagine) teeny, tiny woodland tongue. The sugars provide the squirrel with an energy burst in an otherwise drowsy time of year. Bernd Heinrich, a naturalist at the University of Vermont in Burlington and the author of several nature books, claims that this survival strategy dates back to an Iroquois Indian myth: A youth notices a squirrel licking the sap and decides to try some, too. Acting on curiosity in nature is amazing.

In a saucepan, combine the cardamom seeds or powder and cinnamon with the water, honey, and maple syrup. Cook on low heat until the honey is dissolved. Bring to boil for about a minute to allow it to thicken. Then turn off the heat and set aside to cool. If you used cardamom seeds, strain out the excess and then store in an airtight jar or container.

For a cool drink, combine the whiskey with 1½ ounces foraged syrup, a splash of maple syrup, and barely a sprinkle of cinnamon in a pitcher and pour individual portions over ice. For a hot drink, combine the whiskey, 1½ ounces foraged syrup, a splash of maple syrup, and a dash of cinnamon with 4 ounces hot water in a carafe and pour into individual mugs.

The following beverages are designed to provide a larger quantity option for your family, your guests, or yourself. Store them to pull from throughout the week and engage with foraged goods in a tangible way.

Pine Needle Tea

I've always been drawn to trees and when we moved into the A-frame in the woods, I was instantly drawn to our two white pine trees in the backyard, right along the edge of the woods. Their trunks were so large and the pine arms stretched up to the sky.

Pine needles are filled with incredibly high amounts of vitamin A, which aids in maintenance of teeth, bones, soft tissue, white blood cells, the immune system, and mucus membranes. They have about five times the amount of vitamin C found in a lemon. The benefits are found in all portions of the pine needles, cones, bark, and resin. The innermost bark can be dried and eaten and is valued for its high nutrient content, while pine needles can be brewed as a tea or infused in a liquid for use in a recipe.

Pine needle tea with raw unfiltered honey from the backyard woods and a capful of apple cider vinegar has absolutely incredible health benefits. Ponderosa pine, yew, and Norfolk pine are all toxic to consume so watch out for those and be sure to research the pine you are harvesting from in your area. Connect with your body often; at the first hint of an ailment, this medley will be your fighting army. I believe in apple cider vinegar. I believe in raw honey. I believe in pine tea. All of these combined make actual pure magic.

recipe continues

2 cups fresh filtered water

Bouquet of fresh pine

Pinch of salt

1 teaspoon raw honey

1 teaspoon apple cider vinegar

In a saucepan, bring the filtered water to a boil. While the water is heating up, take the pine bouquet and separate the needles from the stem, pulling them off in the opposite direction of growth. Make two piles, needles and stems. Take the needles and chop them with a knife or herb chopper into 1- to 2-inch sections. Place into the water as it just begins to come to a boil. Turn down the heat! You want to steep the pine needles, not boil them; otherwise they will taste bitter. Simmer on the stove for 10 minutes. Add in the salt, which expands the flavor, and then turn off the heat and keep covered for 5 minutes.

Strain the pine needles in a colander or over cheesecloth and pour an individual portion of pine needle tea into a mug. Stir in the raw honey and apple cider vinegar and sip the woods. Place leftovers in the fridge to cool and use as needed. You can also freeze the tea in ice cube trays and pull them out for smoothies or chilled summer tea or cocktails!

PINE NUTS

The best time to gather pine nuts is in late September or October. Notice the round and open cones and gather them. Remove the seeds and shells before consuming raw or roasted. Pine nuts are incredible for improving vision, are a rich antioxidant support, and have a peculiar way to curb an appetite and help you to stay full longer. They make a curious snack on a hike in the world or on a weekend camping trip. They provide quick access to nourishment, if we open our eyes to see.

Lilac Apple Cider Vinegar Juice

2 cups wild lilac flowers, plus more to use whole

2 cups filtered water, plus 6 cups chilled water

2 cups raw turbinado sugar

1 tablespoon apple cider vinegar and honey blend

Lilacs can be used in so many different ways! Having a party or a play date? Blend lilac flowers to make ice pops or cubes for a sweet, summer treat! Flood edible lilacs in the ice water for a dash of whimsy and color. Bake brie in the oven and top with drizzled honey and lilacs. Bulk quantities can stay in your fridge for about a week.

One of my favorite ways to use lilacs is this simple Lilac Apple Cider Vinegar Juice. Sweet yet tangy and refreshing! Double or triple the recipe!

Crush the lilac flowers with a large stone or mortar and pestle and scoop into a cup, making sure to gather as much of the floral liquid and juice into the cup. Bring the 2 cups water to a boil and add the raw turbinado sugar, continuing to heat until the sugar is dissolved. Turn the heat off and mix in the wild lilac flowers to steep for 20 minutes. Strain the flower petals. You can add fresh lilac flowers to continue to soak and float in the syrup if you like.

Combine 6 ounces of the lilac syrup with the 6 cups of chilled water and a tablespoon of apple cider vinegar. Sprinkle lilac blooms on top. Sip all day.

Woodland Chai

7 green cardamom pods
(or 1 tablespoon
cardamom powder)

6 cups water

5 to 7 star anise

2 cinnamon sticks,
crushed, or ¼ teaspoon
cinnamon powder

1 bay leaf

1 teaspoon fennel seeds

2 tablespoons black
peppercorns

10 whole cloves

Small coin of fresh ginger
(about the size of a
quarter)

6 to 8 black tea bags

3 tablespoons maple
syrup

¼ teaspoon apple cider
vinegar

¼ teaspoon honey

2 cups milk or milk
alternative of your choice

When I worked at the small-town bakery near our first apartment as newlyweds, they had the most amazing herb-based chai recipe. I can still smell it if I close my eyes. You can make this in bulk ahead of time and keep it chilled, then when you're ready to drink, you can heat it up with milk or drink it over ice for a refreshing yet spiced sensation!

Crush the cardamom pods every so slightly with a rock or the back of a spoon. In a pot, combine 6 cups of water with the crushed cardamom, star anise, cinnamon sticks, bay leaf, fennel seeds, peppercorns, cloves, and ginger, and bring to a slight boil. At boiling, turn off the heat and add in the black tea bags (if your black tea bags have paper labels on them, rip them off and throw the whole bags inside the pot to steep.), maple syrup, apple cider vinegar, and honey. Let simmer. Stir occasionally.

Remove the tea bags after 10 to 15 minutes. To serve right away, turn the heat to low and add your milk or milk alternative. To store in the fridge for chilled version over ice or to consume at later date, leave the milk out and combine at the time you want to consume!

This will keep in the fridge for 7 to 9 days.

Pine-Fermented Garlic Honey

Just a spoonful of sugar makes the medicine go down—in this case, the spoonful of garlic honey IS the medicine. Medicine is necessary in some cases, but if I can avoid it, I will. We are believers in the uses of raw garlic, apple cider vinegar, and raw honey in our home, and this recipe combines them all.

This is a super simple alternative to cough medicine and a way to beat sickness before it sets in. The garlic almost gets candied in the raw unfiltered honey (a forager's type of candy!) and is consumed to aid in sickness and boost immunity. Garlic has vitamins, potassium, and antimicrobial and antibiotic properties and the blend of raw honey and wildflower-combed honey has antibiotic, antiviral, antiseptic, antitoxic, anti-inflammatory, and antifungal purposes. This juicy tonic is rich in vitamins, minerals and enzymes. When the glucose in the honey is absorbed, it provides a quick hit of energy, while the fructose is more slowly digested, providing more sustained energy.

We give raw honey to the girls for coughs and sickness. Bragg Organic Apple Cider Vinegar "with the mother"' is one of the greatest liquids ever—it literally has so many uses! I included foraged pine for vitamins A and C and also because I will incorporate this into another recipe 4 to 5 weeks after fermentation. The candied garlic cloves can be eaten raw; the honey can be spooned out to replace cough syrup and even added to toast or muffins, in stews, to eggs, or to an avocado. Nourishment! Hope you try it.

Raw unfiltered honey (enough to fill your jar almost all the way to the top)

7 to 10 garlic cloves

Small bouquet of fresh pine

2 tablespoons apple cider vinegar

Start with a small glass jar and fill it almost to the top with the raw unfiltered honey. Peel 7 to 10 raw garlic cloves and trim off the edges so the garlic is completely edible. Add to the honey. Tuck the bouquet of pine into one side of the jar. Drizzle the apple cider vinegar on top. Store in a cool, dark place for at least 4 weeks. The longer the duration, the higher the fermented healing properties.

This can be taken in small increments when feeling a sickness coming on or consumed as a big spoonful of honey along with the garlic to be chewed and swallowed raw. The pine can be spooned out and steeped in hot water like a tea.

Kombucha

1 gallon filtered water
(unfluoridated and
unchlorinated)

1 cup organic raw sugar

10 black or green tea bags

1 cup starter tea (from
past batch or store-bought
in original flavor)

Scoby

OPTIONAL
FLAVORINGS

Honey

Fresh herbs

Spices

Fruits

Vegetables

KOMBUCHA SCOBY
BLACK MARKET

Kombucha! If you're anything like me, and you love kombucha but somehow die a little inside every time you buy it full price from the store, then it might be time to make it at home. Pine, lilac, black-pepper spice, and fungi'd kombucha are some of my favorites that you can't find in store, and these can all be made from the same scoby at home.

The scoby is the most essential part about kombucha. The symbiotic colony of bacteria and yeast is a squishy cultured mother of magic. The scoby can be made from scratch, but if you get yourself connected to a local crunchy granola mamas group, there is guaranteed to be one circulating. It's like black market goodness at play dates. "Hey," she whispers. "You got a scoby?" "Yeah, actually I just got one from Harmony who got it from Summer who got it from Moss who made it from scratch."

Perfect.

Kombucha is abundant in probiotics, detoxification properties, and energy-boosting elements and is incredible for digestion and gut health. It's a process that weaves both patience and care, and the outcome is satisfying. You will need a giant jar (at least 1 gallon size), cheesecloth, a rubber band or something to bind the top of the giant jar, and a small funnel.

Be certain that your hands and surfaces are clean and free of bacteria.

Begin by bringing the gallon of water to an almost boil so it can steep the tea without making it taste too burnt or bitter. Add the sugar and mix until it is dissolved. Place the tea bags to be steeped in the water. Let cool for about 30 minutes at room temperature or to 68° to 85°F. The longer your tea steeps, the stronger your kombucha tea will be.

Remove the bags and strain any loose teas. Make sure that the tea comes to room temperature. This step is important because heat can kill the scoby. Once the tea is completely cool, pour it

recipe continues

into your jar, leaving a few inches of space at the top. Add in the starter tea. With clean hands, place your scoby into the jar.

At this point, the tea can be brewed as "original" flavor; otherwise it can be paired with a number of flavorings—minced ginger, foraged elderberries, cayenne pepper, fresh herbs such as rosemary or lavender, citrus, kale, or vanilla are all incredible options. The culture will feed off the sugars in the added ingredients and already combined sweetness from the brewed tea, and this is what forms the gases to create a carbonated taste. If you've ever purchased a bottle of kombucha from the store that explodes all over you and basically shoots all over the roof of your car and everywhere—yeah, that happened to me—smile and think, "Well, that's the sign of a well-brewed one."

Cover the top of the jar with a tripled-folded cheesecloth, cotton or linen towel, or clean coffee filter and strap it tightly with a rubber band or string. Place it in a warm corner of your kitchen to ferment over the span of 8 to 11 days. It then can be refrigerated.

Pour it out from the large jar into individual glass jars with lids to seal and take on the go. Feel free to sample the batch—it should taste both tart and slightly sweet. Similar to feeding wild yeast, the jar can be left covered on the counter to pull from, add to, pull from, add to, and the scoby will continue to work its fermentation magic. You'll re-create the sweetened batch of tea, refill what you took from, and never have to buy kombucha again.

NOTE: Save all glass jars and bottles with lids and soon you'll have a small stash to choose from! A small way to reduce, reuse, and store kombucha to go!

HOT DRINKS

The following beverages yield one serving and can be sipped on a slow morning at home or taken on the trail to warm from within.

These recipes will warm you from the tips of your toes to the edge of your nose. They are for year-round adventuring and embracing the magic of frozen tundra or chilled, wet spring mornings. To find ingredients, I recommend local co-ops, herbal stores, or Starwest Botanicals online. They offer a plethora of bulk herbs, powdered mushrooms, and loose teas and ingredients. When making these drinks for packing up and heading out the door, warm them a little longer almost to a slight boil so it will produce enough warmth for you while you're out there!

All of these drinks can be made in bulk ahead of time and even be chilled and poured over ice for hot summer months or warm regions!

Frothed Reishi Mushroom Latte

½ cup organic whole milk

½ cup strong brewed coffee or espresso (can substitute black or green tea)

1 teaspoon reishi mushroom powder

1 vanilla bean

Organic reishi mushroom powder can be purchased at many herb stores and online for around $27 for a full pound, which would last quite a long time! Reishi is antifungal, anti-inflammatory, and incredible for the immune system. This comes to roughly 35 cents extra per morning latte and provides around 77 days of intense nourishment to the morning cup of coffee.

In a pan, bring the milk, coffee or espresso, and mushroom powder to a bubble. Gently slice the vanilla bean down the center and peel open. Scrape out the raw vanilla beans and whisk them into the pan. Continue whisking for a few minutes, then pour into a mug to enjoy.

Frothed Chaga Mushroom Latte

½ cup vanilla sweetened almond milk

½ cup strong brewed coffee or espresso (can substitute black or green tea)

Dash of maple syrup

1 teaspoon chaga mushroom powder

Chaga grows quite slowly in the wild on the side of birch trees here in the Midwest. It contains more than 215 phytonutrients and has 25 to 50 times more antioxidants than vitamin C and wild blueberries. My mom's good friend shared that she was having trouble managing intense continual pain due to a disabled shoulder along with rheumatoid arthritis. A friend told her that she should try chaga tea to help with her arthritis pain. After drinking it for about a month, she could actually feel the pain subsiding to a more manageable level! Prior to drinking chaga tea, she would wake up at night due to the pain in her arm, and now she was able to sleep straight through the night! Please always seek a professional herbalist or consult with your open-minded doctor for recommendations for your specific journey. But, oh, the joy of chaga!

In a pan, bring the almond milk, coffee or espresso, maple syrup, and mushroom powder to a bubble. Continue whisking for a few minutes, then pour into a mug to enjoy. For the tea option, in a pan, bring the water to a boil and whisk in the mushroom powder and maple syrup until thoroughly combined. Pour into a mug with a dash of almond milk and steep your tea of choice.

Mushroom Power

Powdered mushrooms are a tangible way to engage with foraged goods, even at the crack of dawn each morning. Frothed in a morning latte, stirred in a black tea, or taken in pill form, mushrooms have all kinds of possible benefits including:

Antiviral properties

Abundance of B vitamins

Incredibly high amounts of beta glucans, saponins, amino acids, betulinic acid, and natural minerals

Natural source of melanin, supporting youthful looks and vibrant skin

Powerful anti-aging properties

Excellent source of the enzyme SOD (superoxide dismutase)

Supports the immune system

Supports a healthy inflammatory response

Supports the detoxification process of the body

Supports healthy cardiovascular and respiratory systems

Supports healthy blood glucose levels

Supports the central nervous and neurohumoral (they increase the activity of estrogens) systems of organism

May support healthy sleep

May protect against oxidation

May support healthy blood pressure

May reduce fatigue

May support healthy mental function

May support healthy digestion

May improve metabolism, including activation of metabolism in cerebral tissue

Reduces of gout

Maybe a relief from continual pain

Strong Chamomile Lavender Wild Mushroom Latte

1½ cups water

1 chamomile tea bag

1 lavender tea bag

1 teaspoon honey

¼ cup organic milk (or milk alternative)

1 teaspoon wild mushroom powder blend

This calming combination of chamomile, lavender, and a wild mushroom blend of shiitake, woodear, porcini, bolete, and oyster mushrooms simultaneously awakens and calms the body. The drying process takes 8 pounds of mushrooms to every 1 pound of powder, so it's a foraging delicacy. The amount of nutrition that bursts into the system is almost incomparable. If you're feeling extra adventurous and supportive, there are foragers who harvest in their region, powder their findings, and sell directly through Etsy shops online.

Bring the water to just boiling, then turn off heat. Steep one each Traditional Medicinals chamomile and lavender tea bags in the pot for 10 minutes. Pour in the honey, milk, and the wild mushroom powder blend. Simmer on low. Wait for the first signs of bubbling, stir, and pour into a mug! Enjoy immediately!

Caring for Chamomile

Wild chamomile grows along fence lines, on roadsides, and in sunny fields from southern Canada to northern United States to western Minnesota. Be on the look-out for this! Likewise, it can be planted, cared for, grown, and harvested indoors through any season. It makes for a gorgeous winter project, caring and watching for its blooming life and celebrating the welcome of the calmest herb. It requires only a few hours of light per day and craves a south-facing window. Choose a pot that is at least 10 to 12 inches in diameter and has capability for drainage. Tuck the seeds into wet potting soil and press the seeds down, but not too deep. Chamomile seeds require sunlight and heat to sprout. They should root and perk up after about 2 weeks and be available to harvest for tea after 60 to 80 days of growth. Their flowers and leaves are edible and make for a simple yet lavish, most magical topping for a cake, a bowl of oats, or a fresh warmed loaf or just to be gnawed on raw. Calm, medicinal munching!

Imagination runs wild sometimes inside of me and more often than not, I try to find a way to bring that imagination to life. I imagine walking out my backdoor to a giant field of chamomile. I'd bask in the way the wind would smell coming across my face and the sedative nature of it would calm my girls without them even knowing. It's not a fussy plant and lives well with others. There would be afternoons of steeping its dried leaves and letting them infuse in boiling water for 5 to 10 minutes for our ducks to munch them up.

When my first daughter was just 2, I made batch after batch of warm chamomile tea for her. During that long, Minnesota winter she'd sip on the tea and when the warm summer days came, we poured it over ice. It soothed her teething pains and tender, round belly. The dried leaves can be gently turned into essential oils and contains phytochemical constituents rich in plant acids, fatty acids, cyanogenic glycosides, choline, tannin, and salicylate derivatives. This beautiful herb acts medicinally as a tonic, anodyne, antispasmodic, anti-inflammatory, antibacterial, antiallergenic, and sedative. Chamomile is often administered orally or used topically in both dogs and cats to relieve anxiety and inflammation. It may be used alone or in combination with other Western herbs such as mint, wild yam, licorice, and ginger.

The apigenin in chamomile flowers is known to be an antianxiety agent that binds to the same receptors in our brain that mirror prescription sedatives. I am intrigued with this idea that regular chamomile tea drinkers have elevated levels of hippurate, an antibacterial compound that fights colds and illnesses. Let's fill our worlds and bodies with its tranquil qualities!

Just as each single step it takes to care for a plant, day in and day out, the same process is our mental path. Each thought builds upon another and another to form a whole outlook and perspective. Caring for our plants and thoughts takes tenderness, time, and intent.

Chapter 7

DESSERTS
AND DELIGHTS

Dark Chocolate Dipped Fungi

1 cup coconut palm dark chocolate baking chips

¼ cup melted coconut oil

1 tablespoon honey

2 cups foraged in-season whole mushrooms (morels, oysters, hen of the woods, chanterelles)

1 teaspoon applewood smoked salt

½ cups dried rose petals, dried citrus, fresh mint leaves, or cocoa nibs

Coconut palm chocolate is organic and sweetened with the flowers of the coconut palm. Many herbal stores and co-ops sell these in coin shapes that are easy to work with and munch along the way of cooking them down—a sweet treat that is both wild grown and nourishing. The shapes that are produced by dipping the fungi in the chocolate incite a forestlike wonder and excitement that makes me want to get back to the woods as soon as I can. Wrap them in parchment paper or a linen towel. My only warning is to make sure it's not an overly hot day; otherwise you'll have melted goodness everywhere. Store and freeze for a refreshing post-hike sensation or to top vanilla frozen yogurt.

In a saucepan, combine the baking chips, oil, and honey and melt them together. Bring to a boil for about 1 minute and turn off the heat. Brush and wash the fungi gently and carefully place them on a parchment paper sheet. Take a spoon and drizzle and dollop the chocolate mixture over each one like a precise beaver. Or take a fork to each mushroom and roll it around in the drizzle with a tender movement. Or toss the entire 2 cups of fungi into the saucepan and mix it around to cover them in chocolate like a duck slopping in a perfect puddle. These are all amazing ways to do this.

Sprinkle the chocolate-covered fungi with the salt and crushed rose petals, citrus, mint, or chocolate nibs while the chocolate is still wet. Then, let the chocolate cool and harden. Freeze or refrigerate. Devour!

Cocoa Coconut Chocolate Cake

2 cups organic flour

1 cup organic coconut flour (Bob's Red Mill Flour preferred)

1 cup coconut sugar

$\frac{1}{2}$ cup unsweetened cocoa powder

2 teaspoons baking soda

1 teaspoon salt

1 can organic coconut milk

1 cup cold water

$\frac{1}{2}$ cup maple syrup

2 tablespoons apple cider vinegar

2 teaspoons vanilla

Coconut oil

When I was pregnant with our Juniper Eisley, I got into the habit of making a small chocolate cake every Friday. The Bear and I would lie in bed after the girls were asleep, eating chocolate cake and watching a movie on our teeny laptop screen. It was bliss. I baked variations each week, and this one ended up being my favorite. I love the way the vinegar marries with the sugars, making it easy to indulge in without getting that feeling of it being overly sweet. Coconut sugar is lower on the glycemic index than cane sugar or many other refined sugars. It sits at around 35, with table sugar hitting about 60. So it doesn't spike blood sugar quite as much and processes through the body in a much different way.

Coconut sugar is made from the sap of flower buds from a coconut palm tree. The sap is boiled over moderate heat to evaporate most of its water content. The final product is coconut sugar, which is caramel-colored and tastes similar to brown sugar.

Preheat oven to 350°F.

Combine the flours, sugar, cocoa powder, baking soda, salt, coconut milk, water, maple syrup, apple cider vinegar, and vanilla into a mixing bowl. Mix until combined. Thinly cover the bottom of a cake pan with coconut oil and pour the batter into it evenly. Bake 18 to 23 minutes until you can pierce the center with a toothpick and it comes out clean. Ovens may run a little hotter or cooler, so check on that center. It's better for the cake to be slightly undercooked than overcooked because the next day it will be even more moist and delicious.

CHOCOLATE COCONUT FROSTING

1 bar organic chocolate (either milk or dark, depending on your preference)

4 tablespoons raw or regular honey

Splash of coconut cream or milk

I love a good naked cake, for sure. But if you're going to eat cake on a Friday night, you might as well drizzle it with chocolate frosting!

In a saucepan over low heat, combine the chocolate, honey, and coconut cream or milk. Bring to a simmer and stir constantly until the chocolate is melted and combined with the honey and cream or milk. Drizzle the thinnest layer ever on top of the chocolate cake. Indulge.

Pear and Petal Brie

2 ripe pears

1 cup raw wildflower honey

16 to 20 ounces brie

1 cup edible flowers

4-ounce box crackers (I prefer rosemary sea salt or milled flaxseed, but go with your preference)

This delight is made of cheese so warm and soft that the cracker sinks in without resistance and scoops up a bounty of blooms and petals. The caramelized pear is so sweet and subtle and covered in raw wildflower honey, it melts in one's mouth and meets the butter and grain of the cracker like a perfect marriage. Salty and sweet and floraled and warm! It works best to bake this dish in the same pan that it will be served on so the flower petals, honey, and pears do not need to be transferred over. Perfect to serve to others at an outdoor woodland gathering or curled up on the couch on a Friday night with a chilled glass of white wine. Simple and earthy and elegant.

Preheat the oven to 400°F.

Slice the pears into small cubes to make them edible bites to top each cracker. Spread evenly onto a baking sheet or directly onto a flat, round cast-iron pan that will eventually be used to bake the brie on. Drizzle ½ cup raw wildflower honey onto the pears. Bake for 5 to 7 minutes. Pull out and turn the oven down to 350°F. Move the pears and honey to the edges and place the brie in the center of the pan. Sprinkle on fresh or dried edible flowers. These can be foraged or purchased in many grocery stores and farmers' markets. Edible flower options include dandelion, roses, calendula, lilac, pansy, sunflower, chrysanthemum, jasmine, chamomile, bee balm, red clover, marshmallow plant, or lavender among many others! Drizzle the other ½ cup honey over the cheese and florals. Bake for just under 10 minutes until soft. Serve immediately with crackers.

Honey Pies Through the Seasons

CRUST

2½ cups organic
unbleached white flour
(or whole wheat flour,
if you are open to an
even more savory pie
experience)

½ teaspoon salt

Dash of cloves

1 cup cold butter, diced

½ cup cold water

FILLING

5 to 7 cups seasonally
gathered goods
(strawberries, blueberries,
raspberries, peaches,
mulberries, apples,
pumpkins, or the like)

½ cup local honey

3 tablespoons arrowroot
powder

1 teaspoon cinnamon

½ small to medium
lemon, juiced

Butter

Through all the picking and gathering seasons, pies are an amazing way to integrate children into the kitchen. The process of heading out to a strawberry, blueberry, peach, apple, or pumpkin patch can be so rewarding and is an incredible way to show our children the connection of how food comes from the earth to our plate. Studying the growth of that plant from dirt and seed to flower and sustenance can be so simple. Then gathering back home in the kitchen together to bake a pie with the goods to relish in or gift away can teach so much. From picking stems, to peeling skin, to washing fruits or vegetables, to scooping and pouring honey, to rolling out buttery dough—the tangible ways that our children can be integrated into food prep is abundant! I make all my pies with honey and am drawn to the way the flavor of each fresh earth goods comes to the forefront, in an almost perfect blend of savory and sweet.

This recipe is for a bottomless crusted pie. For top and bottom buttery crusts, double the crust recipe.

FOR THE CRUST: In a mixing bowl, combine the flour, salt, cloves, and butter. Slowly pour in the water, mixing it in evenly. Form into a ball, wrap in recycled plastic, and refrigerate for 2 to 4 hours before use. When ready to use, take the dough out of the refrigerator, and gently split into two halves and roll out into a circle on top of a floured counter.

FOR THE FILLING: Cut off the stems, leaves, and any brown spots on the gathered goods. Take about half of the harvest and mash gently. This is a perfect activity for kids and they can't help but smile while squishing it all between their clean petite fingers. Disregard the mess. Stay present. Take the other half of the goods and chop into small edible bites to your liking. The variation in texture and size makes it interesting and delectable.

Preheat the oven to 350°F.

In a mixing bowl, combine the harvested goods, honey, arrowroot powder, cinnamon, and lemon juice and gently fold to mix thoroughly. For a bottomless honey pie, butter the bottom of a pie pan, then gently pour in the filling to settle evenly. Take the rolled-out crust and lay it flat on top. Kindly roll and twist and fold the edges of the crust toward the center around and around until the end meets the beginning.

For a topless pie, place one rolled-out section of crust on the bottom of the pan. Press the corners gently down to sink into the bottom ring of the pie pan and pour in the topping.

My favorite way to create pockets of air for the pie to breathe is to take a butter knife and make small Swiss cross design slits in the top. Five to seven of these should suffice, although feel free to play with your crust creations and go with whatever design feels good. Bake for 35 to 40 minutes or until the crust is golden brown.

If you're feeling wild, empower your kids (age appropriate) to cut the pie before serving. It's amazing to see how their minds work and what shapes will end up on your plate or the plates of others.

Acorn Flour

Peak season for gathering acorns is September through early December. There's a shift in the air, the first leaves start dropping, and it becomes an optimal time to stockpile. Making foraged flour is one of the most rewarding things I have ever made although you should know right away that the first time I made it, it didn't turn out at all. It was your basic, "epic fail" type scenario. I had such high hopes, as I often do. Just as one forages in the wild to survive or someone simply trying to survive their individual world, it doesn't always work out. Our efforts fail sometimes. And that has to be okay. That has to be simply a part of the journey. The process alone wildly changed the way I view purchasing flour from the store. Most of us get to walk into the aisle and view multiple types of flour: gluten free, whole wheat, spelt, almond, ivory wheat. It opened my eyes to a complete obligation toward gratitude for a simple bag of flour and the importance that acorns play within the forest environment.

On one of our trips to the local nature center for apple picking, we perched under the biggest oak tree, surrounded by the biggest acorns I have ever seen, with fresh inner meat and the most beautiful rainbowlike ombre from the base of the shell up to the cap. Squirrels gathered behind us, sneaking in one by one to gather up an acorn here and there and we did the same. I wrapped them in a bundle with my daughter's cream blanket and we carried them home to process.

This process, like all things in life, is about how we allocate our time. An hour spent watching a show could be transferred over to working with our hands or doing something we've never done before. I was overwhelmed in the most beautiful way by how these small gifts filled with small meaty substance could in turn transform into bread, pancakes, or cookies. It changed the way I viewed a giant oak tree every time I saw one. I shared with the girls how an acorn is a seed, and we walked through the life cycle of an acorn. It's the birth of a tree, wrapped in a protective shell or home. The root system is toward the very base of the inner acorn and the rest is complete with protein, carbohydrates, and fat. Close to 100 species of animals including birds, squirrels, black bears, ruffled grouse, chipmunks, and deer mice count on nuts as an integral part of their diet and survival, proving that this process should be done with care and intention. There are more than 58 species of native oak trees in the United States and many more that cross-pollinate. The variation was so visible, even in the collection of nuts that we gathered. Some were short and stout and some long and extended. Just like humans. I love that.

We took them home and our collection came in at just under a gallon. I poured them into a big pot of water to give them a "float and sink" test. The acorns that float to the top aren't edible, either eaten by bugs or already decomposed. These top-layered acorns were removed, dried, and set aside for fall decor. They ended up being tucked into the girls' miniature kitchen.

The rest I gently set in a 5-quart pot to "flash boil," which helps remove the "tannins" or bitterness that they naturally acquire. I cracked and peeled them open to remove their inner meat and found that there was very little "real meat." I attempted to grind them in my blender with around 4 cups of water but they didn't mix well at all. I found myself feeling so frustrated and peeling the inside of the juices and liquids away from the sides of the jar and straining it into a cheesecloth that didn't stay up on the cup and it all fell through, over and over. Anyway, it wasn't pretty. The girls got completely bored with my trials and errors, despite my efforts of singing made-up acorn songs to try and keep them engaged. It turn out to be a beautiful lesson that life does not always go as planned. We moved to their kitchen, the one that was much cleaner than mine, and proceeded to "pretend to make acorn flour" that, let me tell you, turned out JUST right.

HOW TO MAKE ACORN FLOUR
(THE REAL WAY, AS ADAPTED FROM MOTHER EARTH NEWS)

1. Harvest at least a gallon of freshly fallen acorns.

2. Flash-boil them to remove tannins and discard any acorns that float.

3. Grind the dry nutmeats finely by hand in a mortar and pestle or with a grain grinder. Or process in a food processor or high-powered blender with plenty of water (1 part acorn to 6 parts water, give or take) until a thin slurry forms.

4. Strain this into some kind of permeable cloth sack—a fine cheesecloth bag, the toe of a clean pair of tights, or the sleeve of an old shirt with the end knotted off.

5. Proceed with leaching. Attach the cloth bag directly to the faucet of your sink and turn the water on very low. Allow the water to wash slowly over the acorn meal for several hours. In more water-scarce regions, pour cold water into a large basin and submerge the cloth sack containing the acorn meal. Massage the sack initially with your hands and let it sit. Drain and repeat every half hour (or whenever you get around to it) for many hours until the water runs completely clean. Finally, you can start tasting the mush. If there is even the slightest hint of bitterness, keep leaching until all the bitter flavor is gone. This could take as few as 4 or 5 changes (15 minutes under the faucet), as with black oak, or up to 20 or 30 changes (4 or more hours under the faucet) if using tan oak. Use the acorn mush immediately, or store it in the fridge for up to a week.

6. To dry the mush into flour, spread it out in a thin layer on baking sheets and let it dry in the hot sun, in a food dehydrator, or in a low oven (200°F) for a few hours, stirring once in a while for even drying. Once the flour is completely dry, break up the clumps with your fingers or run it through a coffee or grain grinder again if you want to grind the bigger chunks of acorn finer—though if you'll be reconstituting into mush, the larger chunks are actually kind of nice. Store in an airtight container for up to 3 months.

ON THE TRAIL

Here are some quick and easy snacks to hit the trail with! Store in a big jar on the kitchen counter. All nut measurements are described as whole and will need to be chopped. Always feel free to substitute nuts or seeds to your liking.

Enliven Trail Mix

1 cup walnuts

1 cup macadamia nuts

1 cup peanuts

1/2 cup almonds

4 cups whole rolled oats

2 cups raisins

1 1/2 cups coconut oil, melted

1 orange

1 grapefruit

1 lemon

1 tablespoon dried spearmint

Dash of shaved citrus zest!

This refreshing and uplifting trail mix carries you through the budding hints of spring and the heat of summer. Come harvest fall and celebratory winter, it needs extra dashes of cinnamon, nutmeg, and ginger to enhance the baked citrus smell that envelops the kitchen!

Preheat the oven to 275°F.

Chop the walnuts, macadamia nuts, peanuts, and almonds into small edible bites. In a bowl, combine the nuts, oats, raisins, and coconut oil. Cut the orange, grapefruit, and lemon in half and squeeze the juice of each into the bowl. Chop up the spearmint and sprinkle into the bowl and mix.

Line a baking sheet with parchment paper, then pour the trail mix on top of it and spread it out evenly. Bake for 30 to 40 minutes, stirring halfway. Pull from the oven and grate lemon and orange zest on top. Let sit for 5 to 10 minutes, then take the flat spatula and scoop the trail mix into a bowl. Let it cluster and cool.

Secretly Sedate Your Kids—A Fairy-Like Trail Mix

1 cup raw peanuts

1 cup walnuts

1 cup raw cashews

½ cup sunflower seeds

Fresh bouquet of lavender

½ cup fresh calendula

½ cup fresh rosemary

½ cup dried chamomile

1½ cups sunflower seed oil

½ cup maple syrup

½ cup honey 5 cups whole rolled oats

Pinch of salt

2 cups dried strawberries

1 cup dried wild blueberries

This colorful, fairy-like mix will simultaneously brighten and sedate you and your kids. The bursts of yellow chamomile, fresh greens of the rosemary and lavender, bright red eruptions of strawberries, and wild blueberries all blend together with whimsy and wonder. The dried chamomile gets baked into every corner of the mix, and I love the way the lavender leaves merge with the fresh rosemary for an overly uplifting blend!

This yields a big enough batch to offer to others at a party or store away to pull from at a later date.

Preheat the oven to 300°F.

Chop the nuts and seeds to the size of your liking. Peel the leaves off the stems of the lavender, calendula, and rosemary and chop finely. Use a mortar and pestle or rock and board to grind down the chamomile leaves. The fresh herbs and chamomile will shrink and continue to dry during the baking process, but be sure they are still small enough to enjoy in bites!

Mix the oil, maple syrup, and honey with the nuts, seeds, oats, salt, dried strawberries, dried wild blueberries, fresh and dry herbs in a bowl and mix thoroughly! Line a baking sheet with parchment paper, then pour the trail mix on top of it and spread it out evenly. Bake for 35 to 40 minutes, turning halfway through, until just lightly browned. Serve or store!

For a party in the woods, wait until the trail mix is completely cooled, then mix in air-popped coconut-oil popcorn, those adorable square pretzels, and organic dark chocolate Sundrops (see note).

FOR A SIMPLER, QUICKER MIX, use whole rolled oats, lavender, chamomile, peanuts, sunflower seeds, sunflower oil, and maple syrup!

NOTE: A delicious and all-natural alternative to M&Ms, Sun Drops by Sunspire offer great candy taste with no artificial colors, flavors, or preservatives. Their smooth chocolate centers are made with rich dark chocolate, sweetened with evaporated cane juice and a touch of unsulphured molasses, and their bright colors come straight from nature, through beet juice, beta-carotene, and natural caramel. Perfect for snacking, baking, and livening up your trail mix!

Spicy Crunchy Ginger Trail Mix

1 heaping cup raw almonds

1 heaping cup cashews

1 bag smoked turkey jerky

5 cups whole rolled oats

½ cup sesame seeds

½ cup goji berries (wolfberries)

½ cup sugared ginger

¼ cup minced fresh ginger

¼ cup flaxseeds

2 tablespoons cinnamon

2 teaspoons cayenne pepper

1 cup coconut oil

1 tablespoon melted honey

Dollop of maple syrup

Red pepper flakes

This recipe is for all the days you wake up crabby. If you're quick to speak and slow to listen, make this trail mix and then get yourself outdoors as soon as possible, no matter the weather. The hint of fiery draws out all the sass you have in your bones and makes for a quick turnaround of a day!

Preheat the oven to 275°F.

Chop the almonds and cashews by hand into halves or fourths with an herb chopper or sharp knife. Mince the smoked turkey jerky into small edible sections. Process all your feelings through each slice of the knife. Easy now. It's going to be okay. Consider all there is to be grateful for.

Preheat the oven to 275°F.

In a bowl, combine the nuts, jerky pieces, oats, sesame seeds, goji berries, gingers, flaxseeds, cinnamon, and cayenne. In a saucepan over low heat, simmer the coconut oil and honey. Pour the oil, honey, and a dollop of maple syrup into the bowl of trail mix, and stir to cover the ingredients with the moisture.

Line a baking sheet with parchment paper, then pour the trail mix on top of it and spread it out evenly. Bake for 30 minutes, then increase the oven temperature to 325°F for 10 more minutes. Turn the pan about halfway through, giving the trail mix a stir, always bringing it back to an even level. Sprinkle with red pepper flakes and watch them sink into the crevices of the nuts and oats. Let sit for 5 to 10 minutes, then take the flat spatula and scoop the trail mix into a bowl. Let it cluster and cool.

Soft Rose Petal Pollen Trail Mix

Mini bouquet of wild roses or 2 cups dried rose petals

1 cup pumpkin seeds

2 cups toasted coconut flakes (optional)

¼ cup maple syrup (optional)

4 cups quick oats

2 cups sunflower seeds

2 cups melted coconut oil

2 tablespoons cinnamon

¼ cup honey

2 tablespoons bee pollen

Imagine the smell of fresh wild roses paired with handfuls of edible rose trail mix. Nourishment for both the eyes and the taste. The ratio of oats to wet oil will make this an exceptionally soft mix. Baking on low for longer allows the flavors to sink in and chopping everything finer will allow it to bake through thoroughly.

With a mortar and pestle or rock and cutting board, grind down the rose petals and thank them for their life. Be sure to remove any long or hard stems or folds and discard in the compost. Chop the pumpkin seeds.

For the toasted coconut flakes (if using): Preheat the oven to 275°F. Spread the coconut flakes evenly over parchment paper on a baking sheet and drizzle the maple syrup over them. Mix and turn with your hands and bake for 15 to 20 minutes or until golden brown. Pull out of the oven and set aside. (Pair with whole milk vanilla yogurt and a spoon!)

Increase the oven temperature to 300°F.

Combine the pumpkin seeds, toasted coconut flakes (if using), oats, sunflower seeds, coconut oil, cinnamon, and honey in a bowl and mix. Line a baking sheet with parchment paper, then pour the trail mix on top of it and spread it out evenly. Bake for 20 minutes, flipping the mix halfway through. Sprinkle on the bee pollen. Scrape the trail mix into a bowl while it's still warm. Let cool. Enjoy!

Bird Bars

1 cup sunflower seed butter

½ cup honey

½ cup maple syrup

½ cup pumpkin seeds

½ cup golden raisins or prunes

¼ cup flaxseeds

3 cups organic sprouted brown rice cereal

¼ cup sunflower seeds

¼ teaspoon cinnamon

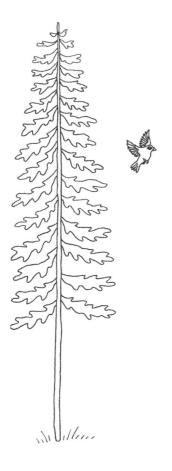

I wholeheartedly believe that when the birds sing, we should listen. In and out of every corner of the world, they are flowing freely, seemingly uninhibited from gravity—they must have a message to share. I've never met a bird or a child that I didn't love. These bars make excellent on-the-go nutrition and are lovely to gift away as well!

In a saucepan, over low heat, melt the sunflower seed butter, honey, and maple syrup. Bring to a short boil, then back down to a simmer. Crush the pumpkin seeds and chop the raisins or prunes. Experiment with this bar by keeping the flaxseeds whole or process them in a food processor for a finer grind.

Combine the pumpkin seeds, raisins or prunes, flaxseeds, cereal, sunflower seeds, and cinnamon in a bowl. Drip the wet ingredients over them all and combine with your hands or a spoon. Lay the mixture flat on a parchment paper square or a round pie pan. Let cool. Cut into small squares. Wrap in parchment paper and string or tuck into a recycled plastic bag and serve on the go!

Earth Bars

1 cup peanut butter

1 cup coconut oil

½ cup honey

½ cup dandelion flowers

2 stems kale

1 cup shiitake mushrooms

2½ cups organic sprouted brown rice cereal

1 tablespoon reishi mushroom powder

1 tablespoon cardamom powder

For the "give me all the earth and dirt" type person, these bars exude the forest floor and provide substantial nutrition for a long hike. Raw, chopped mushrooms, colorful dandelion heads, and curly ends of kale burst out of the bar like ribbons and are my favorite things to experience while consuming this.

In a saucepan, melt the peanut butter, coconut oil, and honey on low. Bring to a boil briefly and then turn down to a simmer. Chop the dandelion flowers and kale leaves finely. Use a food processor if you like, but it's therapeutic to work with your hands. Trim the stems off the mushrooms and chop them so small that you could almost use the pieces as sprinkles.

In a bowl, combine the cereal, reishi powder, and cardamom powder. Add the dandelion flowers, kale, and mushrooms and mix together. Drizzle in the warm mixture and work it all together with your hands or a spoon. Lay the mixture flat on a parchment paper square or a round pie pan. Let cool. Refrigerate if you'd like, then cut in slices to take on the go. Wrap in parchment paper and string or tuck into a recycled plastic bag.

Chapter 8

CONDIMENTS

Heirloom Homemade Ketchup

3 large heirloom tomatoes or 15-ounce can tomato sauce

2 tablespoons apple cider vinegar with honey

2 tablespoons raw honey

2 tablespoons molasses

1 teaspoon garlic powder

1 teaspoon salt

Pinch of each: cinnamon, cloves, cayenne pepper, and cumin

1 tablespoon mustard seeds

2 tablespoons arrowroot powder for thickening, if desired

This is a staple item to preserve and store away to use as a topping for so many dishes! It's very easy to make and is an excellent gift as well.

To use whole tomatoes, peel and cook down over low to medium heat. Otherwise, combine tomato sauce in a saucepan over low to medium heat. Add the apple cider vinegar with honey, raw honey, molasses, garlic powder, salt, cinnamon, cloves, cayenne pepper, and cumin. Blend the mustard seeds in a food processor or grind them down with mortar and pestle and add to the mix. Continue to simmer on low to medium heat, stirring often. Wait to see a slight bubbling, then add in the arrowroot powder, if desired, and stir.

Cool to room temperature. Store in a glass jar and refrigerate. Serve! Dip! This will stay fresh in the refrigerator for up to 6 weeks.

Earth Mustard

⅔ cup mustard seeds

1 cup apple cider vinegar

3 sprigs of rosemary

3 sprigs of thyme

⅔ cup water

⅓ teaspoon salt

⅓ teaspoon cumin

2 tablespoons arrowroot powder

My Minoux loves mustard. At age 2, she asked to put it on her toast and her hot dogs and wants to dip her baked potato fries in it, like any classic 2-year-old would dream of doing.

Soak the mustard seeds in the apple cider vinegar for about 5 hours. Peel the leaves from the stems of the rosemary and thyme and chop incredibly fine. On the stovetop over medium heat, combine the water, rosemary, thyme, salt, cumin, arrowroot powder and vinegar–soaked mustard seeds. Simmer and whisk continually for 5 to 8 minutes. Let cool, store in a container, and refrigerate. This will keep fresh for up to 2 weeks.

Sumac Lime Dip

*1 cup mayonnaise
(such as Just Mayo,
by Hampton Creek)*

½ cup sumac powder

1 lime, juiced

*1 capful of apple cider
vinegar*

Pinch of salt

For this recipe, I absolutely love Just Mayo, by Hampton Creek!
It's soy-free, dairy-free, gluten-free, and egg-free and has a
perfect creamy, rich, and subtle taste of lemon. This dip pairs
incredibly with fish, fries, and grouse tacos!

Combine the mayonnaise, sumac powder, lime juice, apple
cider vinegar, and salt in a bowl. Whisk or fork together.
Refrigerate. Serve. This will stay fresh in the refrigerator for
up to 6 days.

Quick, Mouthwatering Sumac Relish

2 cups petite dill pickles

*1 tablespoon apple cider
vinegar*

½ teaspoon mustard seed

¼ teaspoon black pepper

*1 clove garlic, chopped
finely*

*1 tablespoon sumac
powder*

When I was pregnant with my first daughter, pickles were absolutely my biggest craving. My mother-in-law would call me
"quite cliche," but regardless I would chop them up finely, mix
them with anything in sight, and put them on top of my burgers
or toast or consume them by the spoonful. Oh, to be in a love
affair with a food is utter delight.

If you're a planner and cucumbers are in season, use pick-
ling cucumbers. If you're in a pinch and need that relish faster
than fast, use store-bought or farmers' market pickles.

Chop the pickles very finely in teeny squares. Place in a bowl
and mix in the apple cider vinegar, mustard seed, black pepper,
garlic, and sumac powder. Mix with a spoon. Serve.

For a bulk version of this, double or triple the recipe and
store in a glass container. Refrigerate. This will stay fresh in the
refrigerator for up to 6 weeks.

Duck Salad Dressing

1 tablespoon duck fat

1 tablespoon apple cider vinegar

1 tablespoon olive oil

1 tablespoon maple syrup

1 tablespoon bee pollen

$\frac{1}{4}$ teaspoon crushed black pepper

$\frac{1}{4}$ teaspoon smoked sea salt

Duck fat, beef tallow, pork fat, or bison tallow are all incredible ways to integrate healthy fats into our systems. Spread this on roasted sweet potatoes, foraged mushrooms, toast, or flaky biscuits, or add it to bone broth or roasted vegetables.

Combine the duck fat, apple cider vinegar, olive oil, maple syrup, bee pollen, black pepper, and sea salt into a bowl and whisk to combine. Store in refrigerator for 5 to 10 days. To cover an entire roast, whisk together with 2 cups of white wine and use it to baste.

The Bear's Poppy Seed Dressing

1 cup olive or grapeseed oil

½ cup olive oil mayonnaise

⅓ cup apple cider vinegar with honey

1 tablespoon poppy seeds

1 teaspoon ground mustard seeds

½ teaspoon salt

Dash of black pepper

My husband loves his poppy seed dressing. He loves the way it drips creamily over his kale greens or layers on top of sprouted bread with just slightly crisped bacon and soft, sunshine eggs. It has also become one of our favorite dips for fresh garden grown carrots, celery, or olives!

In a small cup or bowl, combine the oil, mayonnaise, apple cider vinegar, poppy seeds, mustard, salt, and pepper in a bowl and whisk until combined! Dash a few more poppy seeds on top, and pour or serve with a spoon for ultimate appreciation.

Store in the refrigerator for 5 to 7 days. Pair with greens, a bounty of berries, or fresh melons for a cleansing dinner.

Sunflower Blush Dressing

2 tablespoons sunflower oil

1 teaspoon oak-aged red wine vinegar

½ teaspoon apple cider vinegar

1 tablespoon raw bee pollen

Pinch of salt

Pinch of black pepper

Teensiest pinch of raw sugar

An enlivened taste of freshness on every salad, blossoming with summer and gorgeous in color. Drizzle on fresh greens, wild rice, or cooked grains or layer it thinly on a turkey sandwich. Sink carrots, peppers, onions, or seasonally foraged ramps in a jar with this dressing to ferment, pickle, and preserve.

In a small cup or bowl, mix the sunflower oil, red wine vinegar, apple cider vinegar, bee pollen, salt, pepper, and sugar. Whisk together quickly. Pour over A Salad Fit for a Queen (see page 98) or a blooming bed of arugula!

Floral Syrup

3 cups water

4 cups raw coconut sugar

6 to 8 cups floral petals

1 to 2 tablespoons lemon juice

Edible flowers such as dandelions, roses, calendula, lilac, pansy, sunflower, chrysanthemum, jasmine, chamomile, bee balm, red clover, marshmallow plant, or lavender among many others make incredible wreaths, tablescapes, blossoming bouquets, or additions to sage sticks but they also make excellent syrups to pour on top of buttered pancakes, in iced cold press through the summer months, and baked into scones on a rainy spring morning.

Bring the water and sugar to medium heat and whisk until the sugar has dissolved. Pour in the flower petals of your choice, bring to a boil, add the lemon juice, and then turn the heat down to a simmer. Let cool.

Pour into sterilized jars with lids. Put into a large pot of water, bring to boil, then remove the jars to cool. If you don't seal the jars in a hot water bath, simply refrigerate them. The syrup will last 7 to 11 days.

Preserved Garlic

10 to 20 garlic cloves

1 cup distilled white vinegar

1 cup apple cider vinegar

Pinch of salt

1 teaspoon cayenne pepper

A few of my favorite ways to store foraged or grown garlic is to freeze full cloves in an airtight jar, chop garlic in a food processor and freeze in an airtight jar, or chop the garlic and combine with olive oil in ice cube trays and take out as needed for cooking. But by far the best way to savor the flavor and protect the longevity of garlic before it sprouts is to ferment and preserve it in vinegar. A few flavor combinations include adding fresh dill, black peppercorns, foraged chamomile, foraged Queen Anne's lace, or garden-grown herbs such as rosemary, thyme, or oregano. Freshly chopped beets also make an incredible addition to preserved garlic!

Peel the garlic cloves and trim off any browned spots. Soak them in cold water for 5 to 10 minutes.

On the stovetop over medium heat, bring both vinegars to a boil. In a clean jar, combine the garlic cloves, the vinegars, pinch of salt, and cayenne pepper along with any other flavoring ingredients. Cap and refrigerate for immediate use or boil in a hot water bath to seal the jar. Allow it to ferment on a shelf for 4 to 10 weeks.

Acknowledgments

To our parents—thank you for the endless amounts of love you gave through nature walks, unicorn hunts, books, sleepovers, and time spent with our girls while we created and wrote this book. Thank you for your endless excitement and support through this journey. I love you and couldn't have done this without you all!

To my siblings and close friends, I don't deserve the incredible support, phone calls, ideas, recipe testing, manuscript editing, multitudes of messages, and genuine interest you all offered to me through this project. I love you all so much.

To the beautiful online world and readers of *Fox Meets Bear*! Thank you genuinely so much for your support and loving words. Thank you to those who have changed or challenged my perspective in ways to view things differently, for taking interest in us and the way we do life. Thank you for purchasing this book and supporting our family.

Endless thank yous to my editor, Dervla Kelly, who took my beyond-messy conglomeration of ideas and recipes and made actual sense of them. Thank you for believing in this book and grasping my vision for it all from our very first phone call. I am so thankful to you and for your wildly abundant talent as an editor.

An enormous thank you to the team at Rodale Books. Rae Ann Spitzenberger (designer), Anna Cooperberg (editorial assistant), Nancy N. Bailey (copy editor) Sara Cox and Marilyn Hauptly (managing editorial team), Angie Giammarino (marketing), and Aly Mostel (PR). Thank you all for allowing me to be integrated into the formation and design of this and for all of the time and heart you all put into it, which I'm sure I can't even fully grasp the extent of. I am so grateful for you all.

Thank you to my agent, Kim Perel, for believing in the birth of this idea and representing it and grasping the dream for *Tales from a Forager's Kitchen*. Thank you to Olivia Herrick, for helping launch my vision for this cookbook into proposal form and spending so many hours next to me at the computer designing it all.

A huge thank you to Matt Lien, my photographer, for syncing up so well with me on the vision for this. This has been such a beautiful journey to create with you.

Thank you to so many incredible businesses that were woven through this book:

Alice and Ames

Bob's Red Mill

Bodega Ltd.

The Foundry Home Goods

Hackwith Design House

Mercury Mosaics

Mette Duedahl

Minnetonka Moccasin

Rejuvenation

Sanborn Canoe Co.

Schoolhouse Electric

SoftStar Shoes

Traditional Medicinals

Vivo Barefoot

Index

Boldfaced page references indicate photographs.